3

10/13

VENICE

The Doge's Palace

Fondazione
Musei
Civici
Venezia

Texts by
Paolo Delorenzi

Editing and layout
Sergio Brugiolo - Studio Polo 1116, Venezia

Translation
David Graham

Cover
Gentile Bellini,
Doge Giovanni Mocenigo,
Venice, Museo Correr

© 2010 Fondazione dei Musei Civici
di Venezia
© 2010 Skira editore, Milano
© 2010 Marsilio editori® s.p.a., Venezia

First edition: February 2010
ISBN 978-88-317-0656

Index

The Doge and His Palace

The Doge's Palace is a massive but unusual, compact, square building supported at its base by a row of big cylindrical pillars and completed above by a crown of not easily defined spires and arches.

It summarises the entire history, politics, art and institutions of the Venetian Republic. Indeed, it has served many purposes over the centuries: residence for the doge and his family, and his security guards; offices of the various levels and spheres of the State and city's political and administrative life for legislative (Assemblies) and government (Senate, Council of Ten) bodies; place of the administration of justice and imposition of sentences (courts and prisons); offices of the High Chancellor and the State's entire bureaucratic and management complex.

This was clearly not the case at the beginning. It was originally built in the form of a fortified castle isolated by canals that surrounded it like moats and were crossed by a bridge (possibly a drawbridge). The palace appears in this form in the first maps and iconographic documentation on its origins.

The Doge's Palace as we now see it is the result of a long series of modifications, adaptations and partial reconstructions that accompanied the gradual development of Venice's institutional forms and had to contend with natural and accidental calamities over the course of ten centuries of history: the gradual setting out and amplification of the governing apparatus, the multiplication of functions and offices, the overcrowding of the prisons; along with earthquakes, whirlwinds, storms, lightning, uprisings, looting and, especially, fires of various magnitude but always of devastating effect. So it is fair to conclude that the palace is faithful testimony of the history, the evolution and the operation of the Republic, a genuine 'governing machine' that at times operated perfectly and at others was approximate and muddled, but certainly dynamic and vibrant.

Another role played by the palace was no less important. It has always been a kind of grand celebratory 'manifesto' of the Most Serene Re-

9

public, of its glories, its enterprises, its characteristics, its ambitions and its protagonists; in short, its history. No part of the complex architectural structure or the collection of painting and sculptural cycles that complete it is casual. Every statue, painting, fresco, sculpted or carved decoration, stucco, gilding, cladding, fireplace, furnishing and doorway has its own meaning and justification within a programme that was studied and approved by the organs of government. A quantity of masterpieces of art thus enriches the palace, making it an unparalleled monument of Venice's artistic and cultural history, too; almost a museum of exceptional richness and splendour, an unrepeatable anthology of painting and sculpture. More than a 'Palazzo della Ragione', as the medieval comune buildings were known, and more than a royal residence for a prince or lord, it is actually a mirror and weave of Venice, a faithful exaltation and reminder of its incomparable destiny as a city 'risen from the waters'.

The Forms of the Palace

The palace can be divided into its essential parts differentiated by epoch and function. The big Gothic wing facing the quay and the other towards the Piazzetta were built during the fourteenth and fifteenth centuries. These two edifices are almost identical but were built in two different periods, the first beginning in 1340 but interrupted by the great black plague that tragically broke out in 1347. Despite

The Porta della Carta between the palace and St Mark's Basilica

The Arco Foscari, detail of marbles

Adam and Eve
on the corner
between the two
medieval facades

The *Judgement of Solomon*, Porta della Carta corner

Drunken Noah and his sons, Ponte della Paglia corner

this gap of several decades, however, it was wished that they be identical; or that the original and highly cherished module be retained. This consists of pillars and portico on the ground floor, a loggia with a very original series of columns, interwoven arches and quatrefoils, a big wall with white, pink and grey lozenges pierced by big Gothic windows and, in the centre, a balcony with niches and statues. The wing towards the quay contains the immense Great Council Chamber, the assembly hall for the representative body of nobles inscribed in the Golden Book of Venetian nobility. The wing towards the Piazzetta (commissioned in 1424) was originally intended to house the public library, but was soon used instead for the very frequent elections to the various offices of the Republic (the law court had originally stood here, rebuilt in the twelfth century in Veneto-Byzantine form when Sebastiano Ziani was doge).

The extremely ornate Porta della Carta (built from 1438 to 1442), leading into the portico facing the courtyard and the richly ornamented Foscari arch (completed in the 1480s), is the main entrance to the palace and connects it to the basilica. Along with the portico, it is the last great, late masterpiece of 'florid' civil Venetian Gothic architecture. This picturesque setting ends facing the later staircase of honour, the Sala dei Giganti, the elegant, monumental entrance to the offices and the public and private spaces of the palace, and the stage for some ceremonies of particular splendour and solemnity. The Porta della Carta was created by Giovanni and Bartolomeo Bon and has lavish sculptural decorations on the outside, completed above with statues of *Saint Mark* and *Justice*. The capitals on the pillars deserve special attention (particularly those facing the quay, the earliest) worked with figured scenes, allegories, animals, human heads and vegetation. This is a kind of very rich and varied lay encyclopaedia with a resounding range of figures, narrated situations, allegorical representations, astrological and astronomical knowledge, trades, sciences and techniques, and may be considered the masterpiece of Gothic sculpture in Venice.

The capitals, along with the whole range of other sculpted figures – all in the bright, very white Istrian stone that is typical of Venetian buildings – enrich the facades of the palace and highlight its main structural and architectural elements. The corners are thus distinguished by twisting columns and by statues: those of the archangel Michael and of Adam and Eve (on the outside corner), of the drunken Noah and, higher up, the archangel Raphael with Tobias (on the Ponte della Paglia corner), and those of Judith and Solomon towards the Porta della Carta, with the archangel Gabriel above. The periods of these sculptural groups are quite different. Those of Noah and of Adam and Eve are the oldest, attributed by some to the legendary builder and decorator of the palace, Filippo Calendario (executed because of his involvement in the conspiracy of Marin Falier, the doge condemned to death and beheaded as leader of some obscure personal

Venice as *Justice* on the thirteenth quatrefoil towards the Piazzetta, joining point of the fourteenth- and fifteenth-century sections of the palace

The Piazzetta facade

next pages The Scala dei Giganti and the Renaissance facade of the San Nicolò chapel. The end of the Arco Foscari on the left

and political drama); the others are more recent, such as those in the niches of the big balconies (the one facing the quay by Pier Paolo delle Masegne, the one on the Piazzetta by Giovanni and Bartolomeo Bon). The fine, fourteenth-century sculpture of Venice in the form of Justice should be noted in the quatrefoil above the thirteenth column of the loggia facing the Piazzetta. It is perhaps the first personification-representation of Venice as an incarnation of the virtue and principle that were regarded as the very essence of Venetian rule.

Lay, profane and Christian knowledge are all inextricably intertwined on these same facades, the latter in figures and episodes from the Old and New Testaments. This is all typically medieval, so in this, too, the palace is a faithful interpreter of a period – albeit a long one – and a culture. No sooner had a disastrous fire seriously damaged and partly destroyed the wing facing the quay than the question was raised as to how the palace should be rebuilt or repaired. The leading architects and engineers were consulted and gave conflicting opinions. In the end it was decided to rebuild the palace as it had been before the damage. The form - the image - of the palace was so deeply rooted and established that it had become an integral and inalienable part of the city's appearance.

The third wing of the palace is the one that runs along the Canale della Canonica, and forms the eastern side of its inner courtyard. This wing, too, in its current form, is the result of a complex operation that began after the fire that destroyed the doge's residence in 1483.

It has a decidedly Renaissance appearance. Various architects worked on both sides of it, and in the rooms, between the end of the fifteenth and the early sixteenth centuries (Antonio Rizzo, Pietro Lombardo, Antonio Abbondi, called Scarpagnino and others), cladding it with fine, closely worked, highly decorated encrustations of Istrian stone, and with numerous inserts of rare coloured marble, gilding and various pigments, such that these facades must originally have been extremely rich and resplendent with decorations. The signs of the Gothic are here replaced by the typical elements of humanist-Renaissance architecture, with erudite citations and fairly liberal use of the canons of classicism taken from Tuscan and Roman examples, and from those of the Veneto itself. Doges' coats of arms, allegorical figures, portraits, decorative elements in ancient style, brackets, capitals, balusters, small pillars and reliefs are all scattered about inside a luxuriant, if not at times actually frenzied, sculptural anthology.

The fine open staircase, the Scala dei Giganti, is by Antonio Rizzo, but the huge statues of Mars and Neptune (symbols of the two pillars of Venetian power, military might and rule over the seas) are later, by Jacopo Sansovino and were placed here in 1567.

That which we may improperly call the fourth wing of the palace consists of the composite structure that continues on from the Porta della Carta. The Foscari portico at the immediate entrance, a massive struc-

The giants Mars and Neptune by Jacopo Sansovino placed at the top of the stairs in 1567

Scala dei Giganti,
detail of
the decoration
on the steps and
the balustrade

next pages
One of the medieval
courtyard facades
with the
unmistakeable
crown of arches
and pinnacles

tural element with the delicate task of connecting and of containing
the thrust of the basilica's south facade, leads right through to the foot
of the Scala dei Giganti. It was given a fairly eclectic Baroque facade
on the courtyard side (by Bartolomeo Manopola), which contains the
big clock by Bartolomeo Ferracina, a mix of ancient and modern statues in niches and frames, and the side of the triumphal arch that ends
the Foscari portico with its spires, pinnacles and statues.
The Renaissance facade corresponding to the San Nicolò chapel that
looks onto the courtyard beside the Scala dei Giganti (the Cortile dei
Senatori) is of great elegance and richness. Created by Scarpagnino, it
is one of the most elegant products of autochthonous Venetian Renaissance (that is, before the triumph of the architectural language of
Roman origin brought to the city by artists and architects exiled by
the sack of Rome in 1527, most notably Jacopo Sansovino); finely
crafted, with precious marbles, gilding and colouring (revealed by the
very recent restoration), it shows highly effective balance and a matu-
rity of style.

The Museo dell'Opera

Care and maintenance of the building was the responsibility of the Senato at the time of the Serenissima, at times assisted by temporary commissions of experts, and by the *proto* (architect) at the service of the Provveditori al Sale, the magistracy that ensured considerable income for the State, partly intended for the repair of public buildings. The Opera, of nineteenth-century foundation, inherited this technical-managerial responsibility, continuing with the work of safeguarding and protecting the monument. There have been numerous restoration projects over the last two centuries, of which the most comprehensive works to the external facades of 1876-1877 must be noted. Questions of stability and conservation at that time made it necessary to remove a good 42 capitals from the portico and loggia above, and replace them with copies. The originals are now displayed alongside other stone materials in the Museo dell'Opera, taking up six rooms on the ground floor that were once used as prisons.

The figures on the sculpted stones decorating the facades of the palace encapsulate an almost encyclopaedic knowledge, typical of the middle ages, that is rich in symbolic, moral, allegorical and political meanings, with thematic references from the Bible and astrological texts. The centre of Venetian power thus becomes a mirror of the variety of the universe, through images often constructed on the contrast of vices and virtues, the sacred and profane, historical truth and legend, and the chosen home of Justice under divine influence.

Room 1

Bartolomeo Bon, *Head of Doge Foscari*, previously above the Porta della Carta, now in the Museo dell'Opera

Six capitals with relative columns from the portico of the waterfront facade dating from the middle of the fourteenth century are displayed in this room, along with the wooden model of the shoring erected to support the palace during the late nineteenth-century restorations. The intriguing carved representations in luxuriant foliage allude to a mix of astrology and wisdom. The symbology of a good part of the

Museo dell'Opera, Room 2, *Saint Claude*, detail of the capital of the *Five stone-cutter martyrs and three sculptors*, 1340-1355

Museo dell'Opera, Room 2, *Sceptical disciple*, detail of the capital of the *Five stone-cutter martyrs and three sculptors*, 1340-1355

Museo dell'Opera, Room 2, *Notary*, detail of the capital of the *Trades*, 1340-1355

group refers to the influence of the planets on questions of history, read in a moralising tone (*Emperors and Kings*), and forms of life, also with examples of character and physiognomy (*Birds with Prey, Men and Women of the Latin Race, Peoples of Different Latitudes*). The reliefs on the first capital on the right after the entrance show male figures in meditation with crossed legs, who can be identified as *Solomon and the Seven Sages*, an allegory of the liberal arts under the dominion of the Christian faith. The wise and prudent king, engaged in comparing two books, is flanked, in anti-clockwise direction, by Priscian, Aristotle, Cicero, Pythagoras (with a tablet engraved 1344, possibly the date of execution), Euclid, Tubal-cain and Ptolemy, respectively personifying grammar, logic, rhetoric, arithmetic, geometry, music and astronomy.

Museo dell'Opera, Room 6, Columns and capitals from the loggia, 13th-15th century

next pages
Museo dell'Opera, Room 5, *Loggia arch and quatrefoils*, section reassembled with original parts and additions

Room 2

Dating from the mid-fourteenth century like the previous ones, the four capitals on columns show the technical skill of the early craftsmen, despite the ravages of time, evident in the elegance of form and the refined treatment of detail. The subjects of the reliefs range from a series of *Animal Heads with Prey* to portrayals of the *Months* of the year, starting with March, which corresponds to the spring rebirth and the first sign of the zodiac, Aries. A tribute to the art of the stonemason can be seen in the representation of *Five Stonemason Martyrs and Three Sculptors*, while the last capital features the theme of work, disclosing the iconography of the *Trades*. These can be recognised starting from the stonemason in an anti-clockwise direction as: the jeweller, the cobbler, the carpenter, the measurer of cereals and legumes, the farmer, the notary and the blacksmith. Such professions are marked by distinctive headdress (a voluminous beret turned backwards for the masters and a cap for the paid workers, but no hat at all for the apprentices).
Some of the walling that was placed in the last arches of the portico towards the Ponte della Paglia after the terrible fire of 1577 for reasons of stability can be seen against the entrance wall.

Room 3

The most recent capital, dating from the fifteenth century, has baskets of fruit arranged in a sequence that seems to evoke the cycle of the seasons. The complexity of the subjects presented in the other two examples in the room, from the fourteenth-century decorative cycle, is certainly greater and accentuates their charm, presenting these as surprising and sophisticated expressions of medieval culture.
The large capital showing the *Creation of Adam* and the *Planets and their Houses*, praised by John Ruskin as 'the most beautiful in Europe', is from the corner of the palace between the quay and the Piazzetta. The prominent position is a sign of the importance it had within the

iconographic range presented on the facades of the building. This narrates the history of humanity, and in general the universe, starting from the appearance of the first man by the divine hand. The bas-reliefs begin with the image of God seated on a throne holding Adam, infusing life into the just moulded creature, then read in an anticlock-wise direction. The subject then immediately strays from the sacred theme to representations from astrological works, with personifications of the planets to which the signs of the zodiac are related according to their respective houses. Capricorn and Aquarius correspond to the old man Saturn, with the attribute of the scythe; Pisces and Sagittarius correspond to Jupiter, in doctoral dress; Aries and Scorpio keep the warlike Mars company; the Sun, with radiant head, is seated on Leo; Venus, associated with the signs of Taurus and Libra, is looking at herself in a mirror; Mercury holds an open book and sits between Virgo and Gemini; and, finally, the Moon, with ruffled hair recalling her influence over the winds and seas, touches the symbol of Cancer. The other fourteenth-century capital is also noteworthy. It portrays the *Seven Capital Vices*, or Pride, Wrath, Avarice, Sloth, Envy, Lust and Greed, a group completed by the additional figure of Vanity, a girl with garlanded head holding a mirror and with one hand on her breast.

Museo dell'Opera, Room 3, *Wrath*, detail of the capital of the *Seven capital vices*, 1340-1355

Rooms 4 and 5

The two rooms – separated by a wall of stone in big rough hewn blocks, the mighty remains of the building before the current one – contain some column shafts from the portico and a capital with foliage decorations. In Room 5 there is also a section of Gothic tracery from the loggia, a weave of sinuous lines that mark out the inflected arches and four-lobed oculi, interrupted by the upper rosette cornice; the spandrels of the arches contain lions' heads.

Room 6

The stone pieces positioned along the walls, removed from their original places because damaged or unstable, came from the crown and exterior of the palace. The 29 capitals now arranged in the room, originally on the first-floor loggia columns, are by different craftsmen working between the fourteenth and fifteenth centuries (two are eighteenth-century reconstructions). The difference in quality and content is considerable if compared to the portico examples. The decorative aspect here prevails; vegetal elements and foliage fill most of the surface, restricting the space available for the figures. In any case these are simplified and repetitive, such as to make the subject immediately recognisable from a distance, even though all four sides could not be seen at the same time. The iconography merges themes of faith and astrological knowledge to reach a dimension of universal, totalising knowledge, showing animal heads, shells, children, the faces of men and women of various age, people worshipping, others intent on reading or playing music, and warriors and lions of Saint Mark. The original architrave from the Porta della Carta is at the end of the room, along with the sole remaining fragment of the sculptural group that was above it, the *Head of Doge Francesco Foscari*, a work attributed to Bartolomeo Bon. A *Bust of Doge Cristoforo Moro* is similarly the only surviving part of a monument that was in a niche in front of the Scala dei Giganti until 1797.

The Courtyard

The unitary appearance of the external facades of the Doge's Palace is lost when one enters the Porta del Frumento, the current public entrance in the south wing of the building facing the quay. The courtyard took on its characteristic conformation as a result of building works carried out over the course of four centuries, between the mid-fourteenth century and the early seventeenth.

The oldest section is undoubtedly the Maggior Consiglio elevation, built from 1340. It is a flat wall of brick that was at the time pierced only by the ogee arches of the loggia and the Gothic biforate windows that lit the enormous assembly hall from behind. Construction on the Scrutinio wing was begun in 1424, in identical form to the one next to it. It was completed a few decades later with structures taking up the remaining space between the palace and basilica: the Porta della Carta and the Androne Foscari, in which the figures of the Evangelists can be seen in the keystones. The works on the covered passage and the arch, in alternate bands of Istrian stone and red Verona marble on the rear, were commissioned by Doge Francesco Foscari (1423-1457), who is still commemorated in its name. The decorative work continued during the reign of Cristoforo Moro (1462-1471) and Giovanni Mocenigo (1478-1485), portrayed kneeling before the lion of Saint Mark in two monuments that were destroyed in 1797 (a fragment of the first survives, now in the Museo dell'Opera). Some sculptures on the crown by Antonio Bregno and other Lombard masters date from the first period, while the statues of *Adam, Eve* and a *Shield-bearer*, by Antonio Rizzo are from the second; these have now been replaced by copies in the niches (the originals can be admired in the passage near the Liagò).

The fire of 1483 seriously damaged the building facing onto the canal, which was restored by Rizzo himself. Work was begun quickly, but was tortuous and drawn out, being completed only towards the middle of the following century. There are obvious differences between the

The Scala
dei Giganti

The Arco Foscari
from the Scala
dei Giganti

The corner
near the Scala
dei Giganti with
the Renaissance
facade and,
on the left, that
of the early
seventeenth
century

next pages
Looking towards
the Arco Foscari
from the top of the
Scala dei Giganti

part of the facade to the south and that closer to the Maggior Consiglio, due to design changes and the arrival of new architects, Pietro
Lombardo followed by Antonio Scarpagnino. The style of the elevation
is entirely Renaissance in the measured succession of the windows,
the fasciae and sculpted squares, and the slabs of porphyry that stand
out against the white of the marble. A portico on the ground floor
was planned from the start – along which the chronology of the work
is confirmed by the doges' coats of arms on the pillars, starting from
the Senators' courtyard: Marco Barbarigo (1485-1486), his brother
Agostino (1486-1501) and Francesco Donà (1545-1553) – as was the
continuation of the loggia above in the same Gothic style as the
existing one, maintained out of respect for tradition.

The chapel of San Nicolò was built by Giorgio Spavento in 1505,
closing off the Senators' Courtyard to the north, where the magistrates
awaited the beginning of meetings (the *Saint Theodore* from the column dedicated to him in the Piazzetta is beneath its vaults). The
staircase in line with the Porta della Carta, at the top of which the
doge was traditionally crowned, was completed a little more than fifteen years earlier under the supervision of Rizzo, who engaged Lombard craftsmen for the sculptural decoration of the marble. The two
Giants adorning the staircase, *Mars* and *Neptune* by Jacopo Sansovino,
are much later, carved by the artist with the help of his workshop

over a period of twelve years and installed in 1567. The corrosion of the surfaces, though erasing some of the detail, and the loss of distinctive elements such as the pointed staff of the god of war and the trident of the marine deity, have not diminished the expressive power and presence of the giants, who almost seem to guard the palace. The lion at the top of the arch is a nineteenth-century copy of the original, which bore the coat of arms of Doge Francesco Venier (1554-1556) but was knocked down in 1797.

The big windows in the walls of the Sala del Maggior Consiglio and the Sala dello Scrutinio were opened up in the sixteenth century, whereas the portico that runs along both wings on the ground floor was added by Manopola between 1605 and 1609. This architect also demolished the Foscari, or del Piombo, staircase next to the entrance hall of the same name, replacing it with the small facade crowned by a clock that is engraved with the year 1615 to mark the end of the architectural works to the palace, after which it was subject only to restorations. The niches contain some early marbles and a statue of *Francesco Maria I della Rovere, Duke of Urbino* by the Florentine Giovanni Bandini, donated to the Serenissima in 1624 by Francesco Maria II, nephew of the *condottiero*.

The courtyard
with the bronze
well-heads, the
medieval facades
and, on the left, the
Renassance facade

Detail of the
Renaissance
facade

The two well-heads in the centre of the courtyard should be noted
before ascending to the loggias and upper floors by way of the Scala
dei Censori, built in 1525, possibly to a design by Scarpagnino. These
are quite singular in their rich ornamentation and in being made of
bronze. They were cast by founders who also worked for the Arsenale,
an 'Albergeto' (a member of the Alberghetti family) and Nicolò dei
Conti. The latter added the date 1556, along with a portrait of Doge
Francesco Venier, who died that year, and allegorical figures on each
side in sacred scenes relating to water, for example *Jonah Disgorged by
the Whale*, *The Baptism of Jesus* and the miracle of *The Marriage at
Cana*.

The Loggias and the Scala d'Oro

The first floor of the palace facing the courtyard is surrounded by an elegant loggia with ogee arches that continues outside, facing onto the quay and the Piazzetta (and offering wonderful views of the city of Saint Mark). Numerous rooms open up from it, only some of which are open to the public. The fourteenth-century wing houses the offices of the Soprintendenza per i Beni Architettonici e Paesaggistici di Venezia e Laguna; the Renaissance wing the direction and offices of the Fondazione dei Musei di Venezia and, in the adjacent room, originally occupied by the lower chancellery, the bookshop. The main, majestic access was by way of the Scala dei Giganti, but the current route is via the Scala dei Censori.

Many noteworthy stone items are built into the walls. A plaque from Pope Urban V with an inscription recording the indulgence offered for charity to prisoners stands out (1362), along with the precious *Virgin and Child with Angels* from the late fifteenth century, previously in the Magistrato alle Biade. It is flanked by two young shield-bearers with the Mocenigo coat of arms, and commemorative epigraphs of Henry III's stay in Venice, prior to his accession to the throne of France, for which Alessandro Vittoria conceived a very rich, mixtilinear frame with allegorical elements and two caryatids holding crowns.

Note must finally be made of the 'lions' mouths'. Starting from the late sixteenth century, these were positioned in various parts of the palace to receive secret accusations. Notes were put through slots in the form of open jaws or mouths and fell into wooden boxes on the other side of the wall. They had to include the name of the informer, which the judges kept absolutely confidential, and were often addressed to highly feared and very fast-acting magistracies, the Consiglio dei Dieci and the Inquisitori di Stato. Accusations were, however, subject to careful evaluation before the start of any trials, particularly if anonymous but concerning State security.

The Foscari loggia
towards
the Piazzetta

Loggia, 'Mouths' for
secret accusations

The Scala d'Oro

next pages
The Scala d'Oro,
detail of stuccoes,
frescoes
and grotesques

DENONTIE SECRETE
CONTRO CHI OCCVLTERA
GRATIE ET OFFICII.
Ô COLLVDERÀ PER
NASCONDER LA VERA
RENDITA Ð ESSI.

The Scala d'Oro

There is an astonishing profusion and perfection of stuccoes with frescoed panels decorating the vault of the Scala d'Oro (Golden Staircase) leading to the doge's apartment and institutional rooms; a superb triumph glittering with lavish gilding. The entrance at the foot of the stairs is flanked by two columns supporting statues of *Hercules Killing the Hydra* and *Atlas Supporting the Heavenly Vault*, by Tiziano Aspetti of Padua, dating from the late sixteenth century. Despite the arch being crowned by the coat of arms of Doge Andrea Gritti (1523-1538) on the loggia side, the works actually began some years later and were marked by indecision and heated discussions on the choice of the definitive design. They were carried out during the consecutive rule of the brothers Lorenzo (1556-1559) and Girolamo Priuli (1559-1567), whose family crest appears among the stuccoes. The Collegio adopted the proposal presented in 1554 by Jacopo Sansovino, and work on the walls and structure continued until 1559, as confirmed by the date carved into the last side pillar on the left of the second flight. The decorators of the vault, however, were still at work two years later, but the ornamentation was in any case quickly completed. The subjects painted centre on Venus, a native of Cyprus, which was under Venetian rule, Neptune, master of the seas like the Serenissima, and the Virtues necessary for good government. Alessandro Vittoria made the stuccoes, which are arranged to frame and in some cases fill a series of joined cornices. The decorative elements and allegorical figures, many of obscure and undeciphered meaning, in some places appear as sculptures almost in the round, in others seem to only just protrude or are simply engraved into the plaster. The frescoed inserts, with grotesques and more complex scenes, were created by Battista Franco, a mannerist painter who died in 1561. Grotesques, candelabra, trophies and weavings that combine vegetal forms, strange creatures, hideous masks and imaginary animals appear in the backgrounds between the mouldings of pillars and arches, while the two niches in the upper part of the staircase contain statues of *Charity* and *Plenty* by Francesco Segala, with drapery that reveals a study of ancient examples.

ARABIA DESERTA

DESERTUM IRAC

EGY=TUS

Suez
M. Sinai
Pharā
Corondol
Tor
Mubeleb
Madian
Caraz
Sicabo
Chifale
Genamara
Bubutor
Soridan
Istambel
Jambut
Monf
Marzoan
Cor
Hagiefa
Muchi
Remao
Coptut
M. GIANADEL

ARABIA PETRAEA
Eila

HIJ
Hagiar
THAMUD
Faid
M. SALMA
MEDINA
Talnabi
Tima
Jemama
CALPHATUS
Taalabia
NAGEDR.
Naged
JEMAMA
Ballxara

CHADER INSULA
R. ORMU
Kargī
Carek
Rifcher I.
Werdestan
Lara
Ardoil habitata
Baharem
ubi Malgai
tal piscantur
El-Catif
El-Ahsa
BAHAREN
SINUS PERSICUS
Ander viac
Keif
Ju
Voo

MARE
Idhab
Angofina
Veldhab
Buga
Cataractae
Cateracta
Idhab

Vallif Fatimae
MECHAE
Gebel Harafat
ZIDEN
Mucare
Jufama
Mazabiti P.
Mugora
Adiuch
Zerzer
Cor
MECHA
Cariatain
ARA
Miab
Gurex
CHAULAN

BIA
MASCATE
Falo
DESERTA
ARENOSA
MAHRE R.
REGIO POPULI GAD
LOVANGE M.
Prim F
FELIX
SEGER
Niban
Pakir
Meri
Hafec
Pro

Danema
SENNAR
Suachen
DEQUIN R.
RUBRUM
Marken
Erquiko
DESERTA ARENOSA
NUBIA

Traza
Al-Mahjan
TAHAMA San-aa
Cubit-sarif
Camaran
Atfaf I.
Ilacua
Tuice
ZIBIT
Ghalafeca
Babel I.
Moca
Ara
Zeila
ADEN
Laghi
Poe Zeile
Barbora
BABEMANDEL FRETUM
ABISSINIA

Alorf
Scnibam
Elgend
Mareb
Sequire
HADRAMUT
ARTZRAM.
Abin
Ardgye
Mocala
Rochet Prom.
Curia I
Prom. Guardafi

ARABIA
Tigdit
Carefen
R. CARESEN
Taphar
Montel Mira
crefcunt Arbor
Mirabat
SINUS TAPHAR
Farrach Prom.
IN
Socotora I.

TRIERARCUS VENETUS INIURIA TEMPORIS ANONYMUS
ANNO MDXXXVII. TURCICA IN CLASSE CAPTIVUS OBSIDIO-
NEM DIU INDORUM OPPIDI ITA ENARAVIT UT PROBATI-
ORES HISTORICI EUM VIDEANTUR SECUTI ORAS PRAE-
TEREA ET FUNDUM MARIS ERYTREI ITA DESCRIPSIT
UT RECENTIORES GEOGRAPHI VEL NOVIS ASTRONO-
MIAE FRETI SUBSIDIIS FERE CONSENTIANT. EX VE-
NETIS VERO QUI PER AEGYPTUM AUT PERSIDEM AD
INDOS ET MERIDIONALEM AFRICAM PERVENERUNT
NONDUM PERVIO PER AETHIOPICUM ACCESSU IOANES
GRADONICUS NICOLAUS BRANCALEONIUS ET BONAJUTUS
DE ALBANIS HABITI MEMORATU DIGNI
LUSITANIS HISTORICIS

The Ducal Apartment

Ascending the Scala d'Oro to the first landing, then taking the right-hand flight leads across a broad corridor to the ducal apartment, which has always been situated in this wing of the palace next to the apse of Saint Mark's. The apartment was destroyed by the fire of 1483, but quickly restored to a design by Antonio Rizzo and Pietro Lombardo. Decoration of the rooms was restricted to the ceilings, friezes and fireplaces, as each newly elected doge moved his own furnishings here from his family home, which were returned to his heirs after his death. Although located in a highly prestigious building, the doge's apartment offered little space for his private life, considering the public nature of the rooms nearest the Scala d'Oro.

The figure of the doge, nominated by the Maggior Consiglio according to complex procedures aimed at preventing collusion or fraud, stems from the ancient *dux* who governed the Venetian lagoon under the sovereignty of Byzantium. He represented the Head of State in the Venetian Republic, becoming a symbol of its greatness and prestige. At the time of his official investiture he had to swear on a text, the *promissione ducale*, which contained strict laws and precise specifications of his powers. The doge's actions were subject to constant surveillance intended to prevent any personal gain or abuse, which did not end even on his death, as shown by the nomination of a special temporary magistracy: the three Inquisitors of the Dead Doge. Some doges, for example Andrea Gritti (1523-1538) and Francesco Morosini (1688-1694), managed nevertheless to gain considerable freedom of action thanks to their active nature and bold exploits.

Sala degli Scarlatti

This room was once the antechamber for the ducal councillors, whose purple togas probably gave it its name. The wooden ceiling designed and carved by Pietro and Biagio da Faenza (early sixteenth century, with later additions) and the fireplace by the Lombardo workshop

Sala dello Scudo, Francesco Grisellini and Giustino Menescardi, *Nubia, Arabia and Persia*, 1762-1763

55

Enfilade of rooms in
the ducal apartment

Ducal apartment,
Sala degli Scarlatti,
Vincenzo Catena,
*Small altarpiece
with Doge
Leonardo Loredan*

with the coat of arms of Doge Agostino Barbarigo, who ruled from 1486 to 1501, are all that remain of the original furnishings. The sixteenth-century stone reliefs above the doors portray a *Virgin and Child* of the Paduan school, engraved with the date 1529, and a *Virgin Worshipped by Doge Leonardo Loredan and Saints* from the Lombardo sphere. There are also two frescoed lunettes, an early *Virgin and Child* by Titian and a *Resurrection* by Giuseppe Porta, called Salviati, originally on the lower landing of the Scala dei Senatori. The small wooden altarpiece is by Vincenzo Catena and shows Doge Leonardo Loredan with Saint Mark worshipping the Virgin and Saint John the Baptist.

Scala dello Scudo

This room extends across the whole width of the building, from canal to courtyard, recalling the typical central hall of a private Venetian home; it has two big eighteenth-century globes representing the earth and the celestial sphere in the centre. A place for official receptions and meetings, it contained the coat of arms of the ruling doge. The *scudo* (shield) of the last doge, Ludovico Manin (1789-1797), remains above the panelling. The original versions of the maps were made after the fire of 1483 by the geographer and humanist Giovanni Battista

Ramusio, Giovanni Domenico Zorzi of Greece and Giacomo Gastaldi of Piedmont. They were then completely updated with the addition of further paintings at the request of Marco Foscarini (1762-1763), a learned and erudite doge. The work was quickly completed by the cartographer Francesco Grisellini assisted by the Tiepolo-inspired Giustino Menescardi, who added the inscriptions and figured inserts. The maps show countries on all continents, the Mediterranean states, Scandinavia and the nearby islands of the Arctic Ocean, the regions of North America, the lands facing onto the South Atlantic, China, India and Asia Minor. They also celebrate the travels of some famous Venetian explorers, such as Marco Polo, Giovanni and Sebastiano Caboto, Nicolò Zen, who reached Greenland in 1380, Pietro Querini, who was shipwrecked in the Norwegian fiords in 1432, and Alvise da Mosto, who discovered the islands of Cape Verde in 1456.

Sala Grimani

Once used for ducal audiences and displaying the incumbent's portrait, the room was decorated during the rule of Marino Grimani (1595-1605), who commissioned the gilt, carved ceiling containing his coat of arms and the frieze with allegorical figures painted by Giulio dal Moro. The fireplace by the Lombardo workshop, decorated with a bas-relief of divinities and marine figures around the lion of Saint Mark, is surmounted by a chimney breast in stucco added during the reign of Pasquale Cicogna (1585-1595). The canvases on the walls present several images of the *Lion of Saint Mark*. Apart from the works by Jacobello del Fiore (1415) and Donato Veneziano (1459), there is also the famous *Lion passant* by Vittore Carpaccio, signed and dated 1516. This shows a view of the Doge's Palace and adjacent Piazzetta in the background and, with the lion's rear legs resting on the waves, symbolises Venetian rule on land and sea.

Sala Erizzo

This room, like the previous one, is distinguished by a carved ceiling, gilded over a blue background, and a Lombardo fireplace, surmounted by a chimney breast with stucco figures of Venus and Vulcan. This addition dates from the time of Doge Francesco Erizzo (1631-1646), a valiant soldier whose heroic exploits are depicted in the frieze on canvas by Giovanni Battista Lorenzetti with putti and instruments of war. Some portraits of doges by anonymous seventeenth-century artists flank three appealing religious paintings by Girolamo Bassano (the *Road to Calvary, Noah's Ark* and the *Presentation in the Temple*) and a small eighteenth-century painting of *Doge Sebastiano Ziani Before Pope Alexander III*. The hanging garden facing onto the palace courtyard could originally be reached by a moveable stair next to the window.

Sala dello Scudo, with the two 18th-century globes

next pages
Sala dello Scudo, Francesco Grisellini and Giustino Menescardi, *Italy, Greece and Asia Minor*, 1762-1763

pages 62-63
Sala Grimani, Vittore Carpaccio, *Lion passant*, 1516

Sala Grimani, Donato Veneziano, *Lion passant*, 1459

Sala Grimani, Jacobello del Fiore, *Lion passant*, 1415

Sala degli stucchi, or Sala Priuli

Sala degli Stucchi or Priuli

This small room is finely decorated on the vaults and fireplace with stuccoes by the late mannerist Giulio dal Moro, dating from the reign of Marino Grimani (1595-1605) and Antonio Priuli (1618-1623). There are nine paintings on the walls that were originally in the Procuratia de supra in frames made in 1744 by the Ticino artist Carpoforo Mazzetti, commissioned by Doge Pietro Grimani. Alongside some religious paintings by various artists (Bonifacio de' Pitati, Pordenone, Salviati, Bassano workshop), there is a painting from the circle of Jacopo Tintoretto, the *Portrait of Henry III*, who was welcomed to Venice in 1574 amid great festivity on his return from Poland to France to ascend to the throne left vacant on the death of his brother Charles IX.

Sala dei Filosofi

At right angles to the Sala dello Scudo, this room was originally decorated by Doge Marco Foscarini. He had twelve pictures of ancient philosophers that had been painted by Paolo Veronese and other masters for the Marciana Library in the second half of the sixteenth century mounted here in stucco frames. They were returned to their original places in 1929 and replaced by portraits and allegorical figures dating from the seventeenth century. A small door in the wall towards the courtyard leads to an inner staircase that allowed the doge to quickly reach the upper floor rooms where the Collegio and Senato met. Turning around after ascending the first few steps, it is possible

Sala dei Filosofi,
passage towards
the second floor,
Titian, *Saint
Christopher with
the Child on his
Shoulders*, 1523-1524

Sala Corner,
Filippo Zaniberti,
*The Banquet of
Doge Giovanni I
Corner*, c. 1625

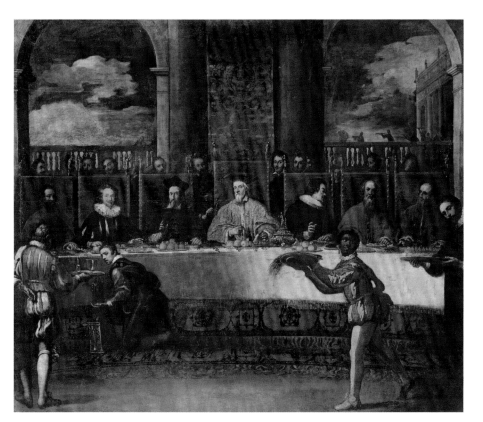

to admire the impressive *Saint Christopher with the Child on his Shoulders* above the opening, a fresco steeped in symbolic and ideological meanings painted by Titian in 1523-1524 to a commission from Doge Andrea Gritti. An early masterpiece completed in just three days, it shows great originality in the choice of having the helper saint cross not a river, but the Venetian lagoon, which can be recognised by the unmistakable shape of the Doge's Palace, Saint Mark's Basilica and the bell tower in the background.

Sala Corner
Lacking any specific function, like the subsequent Portrait Room, this room has a marble fireplace from the end of the fifteenth century with a frieze portraying winged putti on dolphins and, in the middle, the lion of Saint Mark. More putti, along with personifications of the twelve months, appear on the painted band at the top of the walls. There is a family tree of the Foscarini family and a representation of the *Fight on the Ponte dei Pugni at San Barnaba* from the early seventeenth century, a lively scene depicting a 'game' that was fairly popular in Venice. There are also two paintings by Filippo Zaniberti showing

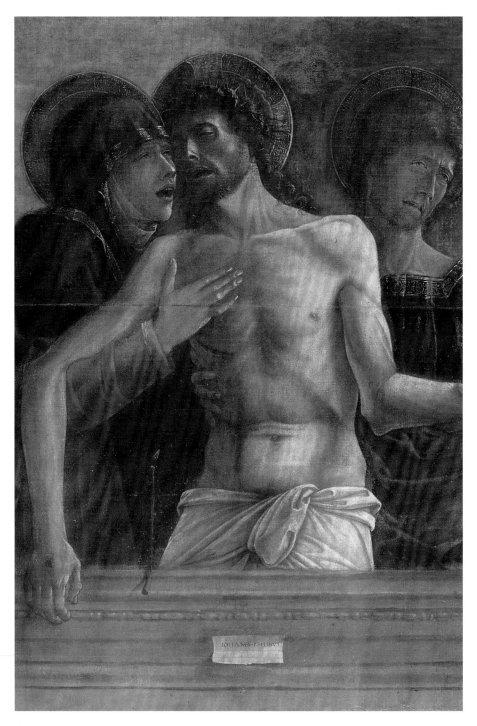

THE DUCAL APARTMENT

IOHANES·BELLINVS

Sala dei Ritratti,
Gentile and
Giovanni Bellini,
*Lament over
the Dead Christ
between Saints
Mark and Nicholas,*
detail, c. 1472

scenes from the rule of Giovanni I Corner (1625-1629), a solemn banquet and a view of the island of San Giorgio.

Sala dei Ritratti

The small Portrait Room has a fireplace by the Lombardo workshop made during the rule of Doge Agostino Barbarigo. A *Virgin Enthroned and Child* by Alvise Vivarini and a *Virgin in Prayer* by the Giotto school are flanked by the famous *Lament over the Dead Christ between Saints Mark and Nicholas* by Giovanni Bellini from the palace chapel. Although signed by the artist, it was probably painted with the help of his brother Gentile around 1472.

Sala degli Scudieri

Once the main entrance to the doge's apartment, all that remains of the original decoration here is part of the ceiling and the splendid doorway leading to the Sala dello Scudo, crowned by an allegorical group with the coat of arms of Doge Marcantonio Memmo (1612-1615) by Giulio dal Moro. There are two group portraits on the walls from the early seventeenth century showing representatives of the school of the *calegheri* (cobblers), painted by Domenico Tintoretto and workshop. The *scudieri* (equerries) from whom the room takes its name, were nominated for life by the doge and provided antechamber services, also accompanying him in processions and carrying the symbols of his sublime dignity.

After passing through the sixteenth-century wooden doors towards the Scala d'Oro, the visit continues in the institutional rooms on the upper floor.

The Institutional Rooms

The sumptuous rooms on the second *piano nobile* in the wing rebuilt after the fire of 1483 were mainly decorated after 1574, when fire once again threatened the building, fortunately causing damage only to this area. Stuccoes, sculptures, wood carvings and paintings by the three greats of sixteenth-century Venetian art, Titian, Tintoretto and Veronese, were arranged to embellish the walls and ceilings of the rooms in order to arouse general admiration, to impress foreign ambassadors and respected guests received in the Collegio, and to perpetually glorify the magnificence of the Republic of Saint Mark.

The gradual increase over the course of the fourteenth century in the work of the Maggior Consiglio, the assembly of male members from all patrician families in the lagoon area, reinforced the authority of already existing and less numerous organs, such as the Senato, with the aim of ensuring better decision-making, rapid intervention in diverse spheres and secrecy on delicate matters. A conspiracy that threatened the political integrity of the Serenissima in 1310 led to an even more restricted assembly being set up, the feared Consiglio dei Dieci, whose action was immediate and very severe. Its wide powers allowed it to put down any attempts at insubordination and rigidly safeguard state security.

Fundamental decisions determining the millennial history of Venice were made in these rooms. The echoes of glorious, now distant times still resound here, where doge and magistrates once paraded through in their black, blue or purple togas, amid busy secretaries and guards watching over the meetings.

Sala del Collegio, Jacopo Tintoretto and assistants, Doge Andrea Gritti Worshipping the Virgin

Atrio Quadrato

At the top of the last flight of the Scala d'Oro, the Square Atrium leads to the areas that hosted the most important assemblies in the political life of the Serenissima. It was updated during the reign of Girolamo Priuli (1559-1567), who is immortalised in the centre of the

ceiling, along with the saint of the same name and personifications of Justice and Peace in the octagonal canvas painted by Jacopo Tintoretto. The eight lateral compartments with Biblical stories in monochrome (*The Judgement of Solomon, Solomon and the Queen of Sheba, Samson Defeating the Enemy Army, Esther and Ahasuerus*) and putti symbolising the seasons were painted by his workshop. The celebratory-allegorical cycle was originally completed on the walls by four mythological subjects, also painted by the famous Venetian master, that were later transferred to the Anticollegio. Religious scenes dating from the end of the sixteenth century are now on display here, an *Annunciation to the Shepherds* by Girolamo Bassano and three paintings referred by critics to the circle of Paolo Veronese, *The Expulsion,* the *Agony in the Garden* and *Saint John Writing the Revelation.*

Sala delle Quattro Porte

A room of solemn splendour that crosses the whole width of the floor, from courtyard to canal, the Room of the Four Doors played a dual role as place of formal entertainment for those awaiting entrance to the councils, and passageway between the meeting places of the Republic's supreme magistracies.

The damage caused by the fire of 1574 was quickly repaired by Antonio da Ponte to a design by Andrea Palladio and Giovanni Antonio Rusconi. The barrel vault, decorated only some years later by Giuseppe Salviati, was completely remade in Roman style, with gold and stuccoes by Giovanni Battista Cambi called Bombarda. The lunettes and ceiling are populated with allegorical figures, divinities, putti, winged spirits, sirens and tritons between rich cornices, festoons and grotesque elements added by Baldissera di Guglielmo, increasing the powerful symbolism of the frescoed decorations and stemming from a complex

Atrio quadrato, ceiling, Jacopo Tintoretto, *Doge Girolamo Priuli with Saint Jerome before Peace and Justice*, 1565-1567

Atrio quadrato

71

iconographic programme formulated by the multi-talented Francesco Sansovino.

They were originally painted by Jacopo Tintoretto (1577), but little remains of his work due to the restorations and sometimes complete replacements to counter age and damp between the seventeenth and nineteenth centuries. The ovals include personifications of cities and regions ruled by the Serenissima (*Verona, Istria, Brescia, Padua, Friuli, Treviso, Vicenza* and *Altino*), while the larger compartments present *Jupiter Consigning Rule of the Adriatic to Venice* in the middle, *Juno Offering Venice the Insignia of Power* and *Venice Breaking the Yoke of Slavery* in the lateral tondi. The canvas with *Neptune Offering Gifts to Venice* by Giambattista Tiepolo (c. 1758) is here as a result of eighteenth-century reshuffles. Previously above the windows facing the canal and now displayed on an easel, it is a fine work expressing the artist's admiration for Paolo Veronese's

examples; *Venice Supported by the World* on the courtyard side is by Nicolò Bambini.

Each of the four doors, whose design is attributed to Palladio and gave the room its name, has a corresponding, late-sixteenth-century sculptural group evoking the responsibilities and peculiarities of the government organs to which the entrances gave access: *Vigilance, Eloquence* and *The Ease of Audience* by Alessandro Vittoria for the Collegio, *Peace, Pallas* and *War* by Girolamo Campagna for the Senato, *Authority, Religion* and *Justice* by Francesco Castelli for the Consiglio dei Dieci, and *Secrecy, Diligence* and *Loyalty* by Giulio dal Moro for the Cancelleria.

The wall decorations, which include votive scenes and commemorations of historic events, were progressively completed by the start of the seventeenth century. The side bordering the Anticollegio and the Senato is decorated with *The Nuremburg Envoys Receiving the Venetian*

Sala delle Quattro Porte, Giambattista Tiepolo, *Neptune Offers Gifts to Venice*, c. 1758

Laws from Doge Leonardo Loredan by Carlo and Gabriele Caliari, to which *The Reception in the Collegio of a Persian Ambassador Before Doge Pasquale Cicogna* and *The Arrival in Venice of Henry III of France, Welcomed by the Doge and the Patriarch at San Nicolò del Lido* by Andrea Vicentino also refer (the triumphal arch was designed by Palladio). Those on the opposite side are *Doge Antonio Grimani Worshipping Faith and Saint Mark* by Titian, with additions by his nephew Marco Vecellio, *The Venetians Conquer Verona* and *Doge Marino Grimani Worshipping the Virgin and Saints* by Giovanni Contarini.

Sala dell'Anticollegio

This was a magnificent antechamber of honour where foreign envoys and delegations waited to be received by the Signoria, along with Venetian magistrates returning from their duties in the Stato da Mar and rectors in the mainland cities.

It, too, was damaged by the fire of 1574, also causing the loss of a map of Italy that was famous at the time. It was restored to a design by Andrea Palladio and, subsequently, Vincenzo Scamozzi. The latter also designed the monumental fireplace with the two marble atlantes, attributed by some to Girolamo Campagna, by others to Tiziano Aspetti; the latter certainly carved – and initialled – the relief with *Venus Requesting Arms from Vulcan for Aeneas*, framed in its upper part by

Sala delle Quattro Porte

Sala dell'Anticollegio, Girolamo Campagna (?) and Tiziano Aspetti, *Fireplace with stucco chimney breast*, late 16th century

Sala dell'Anticollegio looking towards the Sala delle Quattro Porte

Sala dell'Anticollegio, Jacopo Tintoretto, *Bacchus and Ariadne*, 1577-1578

ornamental volutes, putti and nudes modelled in stucco. The same technique was used for the plastic decoration of the walls and ceiling, created by Marco d'Agnolo del Moro in 1576-1577, where a series of scrolls on the vault are surrounded by festoons and divinities, in the midst of which is an octagon with the now seriously damaged fresco by Paolo Veronese portraying *Venice Dispensing Riches and Honours*. The frescoed scenes painted by Francesco Montemezzano at the top of the walls were until the second decade of the eighteenth century covered by *cuoridoro*, panels of imprinted and gilt leather typical of the furnishings in Venetian homes. The four canvases with mythological subjects painted by Jacopo Tintoretto in 1577-1578 for the Atrio Quadrato were moved here at that time: *Mercury and the Graces, Pallas Banishing Mars, Bacchus and Ariadne* and *Vulcan's Forge*; these allegories of the seasons can also be given a political interpretation, symbolising the wise, prudent government of the Republic. The other paintings in the room were left to the Republic by the nobleman Bertucci Contarini in 1713. They are: *Jacob's Return to Canaan* by Jacopo Bassano and the splendid *Rape of Europe* by Paolo Veronese, a highly celebrated masterpiece by the artist.

Two precious, free-standing marble columns support the pediment of the doorway leading to the Collegio, crowned by three sculptures by Alessandro Vittoria: personifications of *Venice*, *Harmony* and *Glory*.

Sala del Collegio

This was where the Pien Collegio met, a State organ consisting of the Signoria (the doge and six councillors, or the Minor Consiglio, with the three heads of the Quarantia Criminal) and the *savi* (six from the Consiglio, five from the Terraferma and five from the Ordini). It had jurisdiction in political, economic, military and legal areas, discussed matters presented to the Senato, heard news from abroad that was subject to State secrecy and received diplomats and nuncios.

Canvases by Giovanni Bellini and Titian that once decorated the room were lost in the flames of 1574. Other artists have left masterpieces alluding to the magnificence of the Serenissima and its regents in a fairly rapid succession of works that give a unitary aspect to the room's decorations. The original wooden seats were made the year after the fire; the rich gilt carving of the ceiling, by Andrea da Faenza and Francesco Bello, is from some time later. The paintings arranged in the cornices, by Paolo Veronese (1575-1577), are grouped into a series of monochrome ovals with scenes of ancient history, eight compartments with the Virtues needed for good government (from the bottom, *Faith, Prosperity, Modesty, Vigilance, Simplicity, Dialectic, Reward* and *Moderation*) and central allegories, whose comprehension is assisted by the Latin inscriptions: *Mars and Neptune* symbolise the power of the ruler ('robur imperii'), *Sacrifice* is the bedrock of the State ('Rei Publicae fundamentum') and is added to never abandoned *Religion* ('numquam derelicta'), finally, a painting with *Venice Enthroned, Peace and Justice* identifies the custodians of freedom ('custodes libertatis'). The painting above the tribunal celebrating the victory over the Turks at Lepanto is also by Veronese, depicting *Doge Sebastiano Venier Worshipping the Redeemer, with Faith, Saint Justine, Saint Mark and Venice* (1577-1578). The room also has some votive works painted by Jacopo and Domenico Tintoretto between 1581 and 1584: *Doge Andrea Gritti Worshipping the Virgin and Child* (a subject taken from a lost original by Titian) on the wall towards the Sala dell'Anticollegio, is followed on the wall bordering the Senato by: *The Mystical Marriage of Saint Catherine with Doge Francesco Donà in Worship, The Virgin and Child in Glory Invoked by Doge Nicolò da Ponte*, and *Doge Alvise Mocenigo Asking the Redeemer for an End to the Plague of 1576*.

The plastic furnishings include the impressive, late sixteenth-century fireplace with *Hercules* and *Mercury*, marble sculptures by Girolamo Campagna, and a stucco crest by Giulio dal Moro in the middle, which shows *Peace* between *Vigilance* and *Loyalty in Friendship*. The passing of time during the sittings was marked by the wall clock facing the windows.

Sala del Senato

The Senato (Senate), or Consiglio dei Pregadi (lit. the 'Council of the Petitioned': its members were in fact originally petitioned by written invitation to take part in the sittings), was founded in 1229 as an annual assembly nominated by the Maggior Consiglio and became permanent only in 1506. It consisted of 60 patricians and a *zonta* of the same number, who were joined at the sittings by the Minor Consiglio, the Quarantie, the Avogadori di Comun, the Consiglio dei Dieci, the *savi* and some high magistrates according to the question in hand, giving a total of up to 200 members. The *savi*, who had no voting rights, remained in office for six months, absolving the important task of preparing the business to be presented during the assemblies and supervising implementation of the *parti* (laws). The matters dealt with ranged from general and foreign policy to administration of the mainland, military and naval questions, maritime trade and control of the Arsenale.

This room did not escape the fire of 1574, either, but was quickly restored under the direction of Antonio da Ponte. The work began with the wooden tribune and ceiling, by the same craftsmen working in the Collegio: Andrea da Faenza and Francesco Bello, to a design by the cartographer and decorator Cristoforo Sorte. The works continued for several years, as shown by the coat of arms of Doge Pasquale Cicogna (1585-

1595) amid the elaborate gilt wood carving. A canvas by Jacopo and Domenico Tintoretto showing *The Triumph of Venice* is in the middle, surrounded by works glorifying the power and virtues of the Republic by various artists (Palma Giovane, Andrea Vicentino, Antonio Aliense, Marco Vecellio, Tommaso Dolabella and Girolamo Gambarato).

The walls of the room, which were originally decorated with a series of maps by Cristoforo Sorte showing the entire extent of Venetian rule, are adorned by two clocks, one of which shows the signs of the zodiac, and by allegorical scenes and votive pictures from the late sixteenth century. Above the tribunal is a painting of the *Dead Christ Supported by Angels and Worshipped by Doges Pietro Lando and Marcantonio Trevisan* by Jacopo Tintoretto and workshop, facing a canvas by Palma Giovane with *Doges Lorenzo and Girolamo Priuli Worshipping Christ Triumphant*. The Basilica of Saint Mark appears in the background of another work by Tintoretto at the side: *Doge Pietro Loredan Kneeling Before the Virgin*, which is followed by *Doge Pasquale Cicogna Entreating Christ* and *Doge Francesco Venier Presenting the Subject Cities to Venice* by Palma Giovane. The latter also painted the singular representation at the entrance to the Collegio, the *Allegory of the League of Cambrai*, celebrating the Republic's victory over the anti-Venetian coalition in 1508: Europe, mounted on an angry bull, is about to hurl itself against a young woman with a sword, the personification of the Serenissima, who is spurred on by Doge Leonardo Loredan, while

Sala del Collegio

Sala del Collegio,
ceiling, Paolo
Veronese, *Dialectic*,
1575-1577

two winged victories carry palm branches and crowns of laurel. Finally, between the windows, there is a painting with *Saint Lorenzo Giustiniani Giving the Benediction at San Pietro di Castello* by Marco Vecellio.

The decorations in the room were completed in 1775 when the two monochromes by Giandomenico Tiepolo with ancient examples of rhetorical skills were added at the sides of the throne: *Demosthenes' Oration Against Eschinus* and *Cicero's Oration Against Catiline*.

Sala del Consiglio dei Dieci

The discontent aroused in those excluded by the *serrata* of the Maggior Consiglio (1297) gave rise, thirteen years later, to the conspiracy of Baiamonte Tiepolo and Marco Querini, severely repressed by the State authority. In order to punish the guilty and prevent new attacks, it was decided to nominate a special, temporary commission, the Consiglio dei Dieci (Council of Ten), which was then regularly re-newed until being made permanent in 1455. The sittings, in which the Ten, the Minor Consiglio and at least one Avogadore di Comun took part, ensuring respect for the law (until 1582 there was also a *zonta* of fifteen patricians), were held in the utmost privacy. This was necessitated by the assembly's delicate tasks pertaining to the calm and prosperity of the State, public order, penalties for political offences or those committed by nobles and the moral and good be-haviour of the public. In order to achieve such aims, the magistrates could make use of the inquisitorial rite, which also allowed torture, characterised by the secrecy of the verdict and the irrevocable nature of the sentence.

The wooden panelling along the perimeter of the room is original, but the seats are missing from the semi-circular tribune, to the right of which there is a hidden door leading to the offices behind and a

Sala del Collegio, ceiling, Paolo Veronese, *Mars and Neptune*, 1575-1577

Sala del Senato

staircase to the places of detention. A frieze by Giambattista Zelotti runs around the top of the walls with putti, allegorical figures and the coat of arms of Doge Francesco Donà (1545-1553); lower down there are canvases dating from the late sixteenth or early seventeenth century: at the end *The Adoration of the Magi* by Antonio Aliense, at the sides *The Bologna Peace between Charles V and Clement VII in 1530* by Marco Vecellio and *The Meeting of Pope Alexander III and Doge Sebastiano Ziani After the Battle of Salvore* by Francesco and Leandro Bassano. There are some very interesting pictorial decorations between carved festoons on the ceiling, painted in 1553-1554 on the basis of an iconographic programme directed by the noble scholar Daniele Barbaro. Giambattista Ponchino da Castelfranco was invited to paint the compartments, and chose the twenty-five-year-old Paolo Veronese as his assistant, who in turn involved his companion and follower Giambattista Zelotti in the work. The frames enclose a series of chiaroscuri of allegorical and symbolic subject (virile nudes at the corners, four impressive female figures nearer the centre), around larger panels, of alternately oval and rectangular shape, with divinities and representations intended to glorify the magnificence of the Republic. The elliptical

Sala del Senato, Jacopo Palma Giovane, *Allegory of the League of Cambrai*, 1590-1595

Sala del Senato, *Clock*, end of 16th century

next pages
Sala del Senato, detail of carved and gilt ceiling frames

Sala del Consiglio
dei Dieci, ceiling,
Paolo Veronese,
*Oriental Elder
and Young Woman*,
1553-1554

Sala del Consiglio
dei Dieci, ceiling,
Paolo Veronese,
*Venice Receiving
Riches and
Honours from Juno*,
1553-1554

insert with an *Oriental Elder and Young Woman*, and the vertical picture portraying *Venice Receiving Riches and Honours from Juno* are certainly by Veronese, as is the central painting showing *Jupiter Banishing the Vices*, though this is a copy as the original was taken away by the French in 1797 (the original is in the Louvre). The Olympic divinity is a metaphor for the Consiglio dei Dieci, which, availing itself of the winged spirit with the book of decrees, opposes the most savage and pernicious crimes.

This room and the subsequent Sala della Bussola are situated in the part of the palace built in the second quarter of the sixteenth century by Scarpagnino.

Sala della Bussola

The painting in the centre of the ceiling portraying *Saint Mark Crowning the Theological Virtues* is a nineteenth-century copy of the original by Paolo Veronese (1554), which was stolen by the French in 1797 and is now exhibited in the Louvre. The fireplace supported by two atlantes, designed by Jacopo Sansovino and made by his students Danese Cattaneo and Pietro da Salò, presents the insignia of Doge Marcantonio Trevisan (1553-1554). The room is further enhanced by seventeenth-century paintings by Antonio Aliense (allegorical images, conquests of cities) and Marco Vecellio, who painted the four votive pictures showing *The Virgin Worshipped by Doge Leonardo Donà* (1606-1612). The big revolving wooden door (*bussola*) in the corner, which gives access to hidden passages, is crowned by a statue of *Justice* with

sword and scales. Indeed, the room was an antechamber to the supreme
court of the Republic, the Consiglio dei Dieci, for witnesses, defence
counsels and the accused, and also adjoins the rooms of the Tre Capi
and the Inquisitors (included on the Secret Itinerary tour). The places
where the magistracies with judicial functions sat were connected by
internal stairways that crossed through the palace from the wells on
the ground floor to the leads in the attic. The *bocca di leone* next to
the door leading to the Scala dei Censori was used to collect anonymous accusations, and is the only one in the palace to have retained
its original wooden hatches and locks, which were opened with keys
held by three different officials.

On leaving the room, take the corridor on the right to go to the
Armeria.

The Armeria

An armoury was already part of the Byzantine building raised by Doge Sebastiano Ziani (1172-1178). When the new fourteenth-century wing was built, it was firstly located in the so-called Sala dell'Armamento, near the Maggior Consiglio, and slightly later in the upper rooms that had until then been used to confine prisoners of a certain prestige. Documents show that this area was known as the 'Torresella', recalling one of the towers of the earlier ducal castle that rose on precisely this site.

Initially under the control of the Maggior Consiglio, the Armeria was subsequently entrusted to the Consiglio dei Dieci, whose initials 'CX' or the lion of Saint Mark appear on the entrance locks and many of the pieces kept in the rooms, such as shields and quivers. The collections grew over the centuries with relics, war booty, standards, trophies, fabrics, sculptures and paintings donated to the State, giving it not only a functional role but also a representative one, such that it was especially opened for high ranking visitors like Henry III.

When the assembly of the entire patrician body of the Serenissima sat, firearms were loaded and swords drawn by the body guards who ensured its correct procedure. In the meantime, a procurator of Saint Mark checked the piazza from the loggia of the bell tower with a chosen group of Arsenalotti, the loyal, specialist craftsmen who worked in the Arsenale and were also assigned the task of protecting the palace on the days following the death of a doge.

Although sacked after the fall of the Republic in 1797, the collection still contains more than 2000 arms of various form and mechanism.

Room 1

Five precious suits of armour for battles or tournaments dating from the sixteenth century are displayed next to the entrance, surrounded by pikes and falchions on long poles. According to a tradition since refuted on typological and chronological grounds, the finely tooled, gilt decorated example with a cat's head and wolf profiles belonged to Erasmo da Narni, called Gattamelata, *capitano generale* of the Venetian armies from 1437. Alongside is a suit of horse's armour that belonged to Francesco Doudo, a heroic warrior at Lepanto and in the war of Candia, along with a small cuirass for a dwarf, or perhaps used to train a child, that is said to have been found in 1515 on the battlefield of Marignano. In the showcase next to the door of the following room there are two important Milanese suits of tournament armour dating from around 1490, and a lighter brigandine used for fighting on foot. The room also contains some morions, sixteenth-century, pointed steel helmets, along with models of arms, swords from various periods, crossbows and quivers in painted or printed leather for holding arrows. The flags and two ship's lanterns with the Turkish crescent are spoils of war.

Armeria, Room 2, The armour of Henry IV of France, donated to the Republic in 1604

Room 2

A rectangular Ottoman standard captured at Lepanto in 1571 hanging from the ceiling has verses from the Koran embroidered along the edges and an inscription praising Allah and the prophet Muhammad in the centre. The arms on display exemplify the variety of forms and the external refinement developed in offensive weapons and protective cuirasses over the centuries: swords and two-handled broadswords for slashing in battle, insidious fire halberds, shields (bucklers, parade shields) and numerous helmets (sallets, crested morions, a parade basinet from around 1480), along with a metal harness for a horse's head. In the centre of a marble niche on the end wall is the armour Henry IV of France donated to the Republic in 1604, which clearly shows the dent made by the test shot fired to prove its strength. The small room behind has swords, shields and morions; its original use as a prison (the so-called 'Torresella') is confirmed by inscriptions left on the plaster by prisoners held here.

Room 3

The showcase along the wall of the room has an outstanding range of arms: halberds, pikes, spears, falchions, crossbows, quivers and shields (some with the initials of the Consiglio dei Dieci or the lion of Saint Mark), morions, swords and clubs. Outside this there is a seventeenth-century harquebus with twenty barrels, similar to a modern machine gun, a fuse box in perforated, embossed copper (1521) and a culverin, or small cannon, from the sixteenth century. The bronze bust of Francesco Morosini, future doge, overlooks the whole collection from a niche on a base of war trophies. It was commissioned by the Senato in 1687 from the Genoese sculptor Filippo Parodi to celebrate the merits of this person known as 'il Peloponnesiaco' for his conquests and victories against the Turks in that part of Greece. The proud soldier holds the rod of command and wears the typical garments of

HENRICI IV FRANCIÆ ET NAVARÆ REGIS ARMA
IN TOT TANTISQ ET PERICVLIS ET VICTORIIS HOSTILI
SANGVINE MADEFACTA IMMORTALIS EIVS GLORIÆ TROPHÆVM
AC VERI ET SINCERI AMORIS ERGA REMPVB
MONVMENTVM

a *capitano generale da Mar*: the cuirass, the cape held on the right shoulder by five *peroli* (buttons) and the *a tozzo* headgear. In 1694 he was dedicated another monument, the triumphal arch in the Sala dello Scrutinio.

Room 4

This room is in the southern corner of the palace, with windows overlooking the basin. It has a varied display of mixed arms, mainly pistols, harquebuses with fuse and striker (some were donated by a Persian ambassador to Doge Marino Grimani in 1602), gunpowder flasks, broadswords, clubs, crossbows and two fifteenth-century papal rapiers. There are also arms that were particularly insidious because of their small size and thus prohibited, which came from the Carrara family, lords of Padua, who were defeated by the Venetians in 1405. There is then also a chastity belt, instruments of torture and lethal devices, such as an iron key with concealed spike, a small poisoned die and the 'devil's box', fitted with four pistol barrels inside that fired when it was opened. There are two bronze busts by Tiziano Aspetti dating from the late sixteenth century in the room, immortalising Agostino Barbarigo, wounded in the Battle of Lepanto, and Marcantonio Bragadin, the heroic defender of Famagosta who was flayed by the Turks in 1571 (his skin, taken to Constantinople, was recovered a few years later by a young seaman and is now kept in the church of Santi Giovanni e Paolo).

The previous rooms must be retraced to reach the exit from the Armeria, after which there is a short staircase overlooked by a canvas with the lion of Saint Mark and a marble bust of the Venetian admiral at Lepanto, Sebastiano Venier, sculpted and left to the Republic by Alessandro Vittoria in 1608. The wooden doors date from 1556 and were made from precious planks of cedar brought especially from Lebanon.

Maggior Consiglio and Scrutinio

The unique Venetian republican system required the entire patrician class to take part in the administration of power, dispensed among its members by a complex system of ballots and defaults.

The families of the nobility in the lagoon area were divided into four classes: the so-called *case vecchie*, which were already in control at the earliest times, the *case nuove*, which appeared after 800, the *case nuovissime*, which were selected from among the optimates at the time of the war of Chioggia (1380), and finally the houses that purchased their noble titles during the wars of Candia and Morea, between the mid-seventeenth century and the start of the eighteenth. Another distinction was made shortly before the close of Venice's historic parabola, based on financial status and the responsibilities usually taken on by members of the various aristocratic families, thus adding *senatorie*, *giudiziarie* and *barnabotte* (in the parish of San Barnaba there were lodgings let by the State at low rentals) to the chosen elite. The Maggior Consiglio (Great Council) was descended from the original Comune's organs of government and, after the *serrata* of 1297, became the hereditary body to which all nobles born legitimately and not taking up an ecclesiastical career were admitted from the age of 25 (or 20 if included among those chosen by lot on Saint Barbara's Day). Their various privileges included the right to grant pardons and to recommend officials for the Republic's numerous magistracies. Elections took place in the Sala dello Scrutinio (Voting Chamber) and were very laborious, reaching the greatest degree of complexity in the procedures for appointing a doge. A ballot was placed in the urn for each noble of the Maggior Consiglio, and a scroll marked with the word 'lector' inserted in 30 of these. Nine names were initially drawn to elect 40 others, from whom 12 where chosen by lot. These 12 then elected 25 members, from whom nine were chosen by lot; the nine then elected 45, reduced by lot to 11. These 11 voters then nominated the 41 electors of the Doge.

Sala del Maggior Consiglio, ceiling, Jacopo Tintoretto and assistants, *Doge Nicolò da Ponte, in the Presence of Venice, Receiving Tribute from the Ambassadors of the Subject Cities*, detail, 1584

It was a kind of aristocratic democracy that restricted excessive individualism to deter abuses of power or malfeasance, and was for centuries able to proudly maintain Venetian *libertas*, holding its head high with kings, emperors and popes.

Liagò

The next room after visiting the second floor is the Liagò (a Venetian term meaning veranda, an illuminated passageway), which once acted as an antechamber during sittings of the Maggior Consiglio. The ceiling with gilt beams dates from the end of the sixteenth century, while the arrangement of paintings dates from the early seventeenth century, with works by Domenico Tintoretto (*The Sea People Offering a Model of a Galley to Saint Justine, The Transfiguration* and *Doge Giovanni Bembo Before Venice with Allegorical Figures*, on the left) and Palma Giovane (*Doge Marcantonio Memmo Before the Virgin with Symbolic Figures of Subject Cities* between *Religion* and *Concord*, on the opposite side). The nearby vestibule has a preparatory cartoon by Sebastiano Ricci for the mosaic of the second external doorway in the facade of the basilica showing *The Arrival of the Body of Saint Mark in Venice*, and three sculptures by Antonio Rizzo, *Adam, Eve* and the *Shield-bearer*, made between 1462 and 1471 to decorate the Foscari Arch, where

Liagò,

Liagò, Antonio Rizzo, *Adam and Eve*, 1462-1471

they are now replaced by copies. The windows looking onto the Basin still have the multi-lancets and marble quatrefoils that were elsewhere destroyed by the fire of 1577 and never replaced.

Quarantia Civil Vecchia

A magistracy of very early institution (it may have already been functioning at the end of the twelfth century), the Consiglio dei Quaranta (Council of Forty) had jurisdiction over legal matters, with such vast responsibilities that at the beginning of the fifteenth century it had to be divided into three distinct assemblies: the Quarantia Criminale for penal matters, and the Quarantia Civil Vecchia and Quarantia Civil Nuova to deal with trials and appeals, one for Venice and the other for the mainland.

The room took on its present appearance in the seventeenth century and is dominated by the big Gothic window on the canal side. It still has a fragment of fresco behind the wooden panelling to the right of the entrance in which it is easy to recognise the outline of Saint Mark's Basilica. The canvases, hung on the walls between the second and fourth decades of the seventeenth century, portray sacred scenes in celebration of the Serenissima. A votive shrine dedicated to the Virgin is placed at the centre of the work by Pietro Malombra with *Venice Accepting the Supplications of the Citizens*, which is followed by *Venice Receiving the Sceptre of Rule* by Giovanni Battista Lorenzetti above the entrance, *Moses Destroying the Golden Calf,* the *Massacre of the Idolatrous Jewish People* and, on the arch, the *Annunciation* by Andrea Celesti.

Sala dell'Armamento or del Guariento

This small room, divided in early times into two floors and connected to the rooms above by stairs, was intended as an ammunition store, but also as a waiting room for the armed guard that watched over the sittings of the Maggior Consiglio, ready to intervene if necessary. It

Sala dell'Armamento,
Jacopo Tintoretto
(attributed), *Model
for the Paradise,
after* 1582 (on loan
from the IRE, Venice)

Sala dell'Armamento,
Guariento,
*Coronation of
the Virgin*, detail,
1365-1368

next pages
Sala del Maggior
Consiglio, Jacopo
and Domenico
Tintoretto, *Paradise*,
detail, 1588-1594

Sala del Maggior
Consiglio

Sala del Maggior
Consiglio, ceiling,
Paolo Veronese,
Triumph of Venice,
1582

now houses the remains of the big fourteenth-century fresco by Guariento, devastated by fire in 1577; this was found under Tintoretto's *Paradise* and detached in 1903. The work dates back to the reign of Marco Corner (1365-8) and shows the *Coronation of the Virgin*, enthroned beside the Redeemer, while hosts of angels, the Evangelists, blessed, patriarchs and prophets all crowd around in worship. The fresco depicts the Annunciation at the ends (Mary on the right, the Archangel on the left), and was enriched by gold and silver ornamentation, with epigraphs that are now almost completely lost.

Sala del Maggior Consiglio
The wing of the palace looking onto the basin is almost entirely taken up by the very large assembly hall of the Maggior Consiglio (Great Council), which is more than 50 metres long and almost 25 wide. The doge sat at the centre of the tribunal among the councillors, surrounded by the three heads of the Consiglio dei Dieci, the Quarantia Criminale, the Avogadori di Comun and the censors, while the nobles sat around the hall on high-backed chairs at the sides and double benches arranged in nine rows. The Maggior Consiglio, which had turned into a hereditary assembly after the *serrata* of 1297, gradually delegated many duties to reformed or newly created magistracies to ensure better administration of public affairs. But the assembly in

HIC EST LOCVS MARINI FALETRO DECAPITATI PRO CRIMINIBVS

any case reserved the right to elect the members of the numerous offices that did not come under the jurisdiction of the Senato (so-called 'distributive justice') and, in theory at least, maintained supreme authority over legislative matters until 1797.

Although the building was certainly decorated from as early as the twelfth century, the current building, raised quickly from 1340, was decorated in three distinct periods. All that remains of the first of these, completed at the start of the fifteenth century, are fragments of Guariento's fresco of *Paradise* (or the *Coronation of the Virgin*, considering the importance of the scene in the remaining part of the work now displayed in the Sala dell'Armamento), while the historic figures painted by Gentile da Fabriano, Pisanello and Antonio Veneziano, possibly also Michelino da Besozzo, were lost in just a few decades due to damp. It was therefore necessary to replace the decorations, duly carried out between 1474 and 1564 by Alvise Vivarini, Gentile and Giovanni Bellini, Carpaccio, Titian (the celebrated *Battle of Spoleto*), Pordenone, Tintoretto and Veronese. But these works were also abruptly lost among the flames of the devastating fire of 1577.

Although some, including Palladio, proposed demolishing the still smoking remains of the palace to build a modern replacement, it was eventually decided to keep and restore the fourteenth-century structures on the basis of a plan presented by Giovanni Antonio Rusconi. Three years later the Maggior Consiglio was able to resume its sittings in the hall, but this remained bare as the major task of decorating it was not completed until the start of the seventeenth century. It was decided not to restore the golden, star-covered sky dating from the rule of Michele Steno (1400-1413), in favour of a more updated intaglio ceiling, designed by Cristoforo Sorte, so as to increase the space available for celebration of the 'myth' of Venice, an inviolate and favoured city in the eyes of God. Jacopo Contarini and Jacopo Marcello, two patrician experts in painting and history, drafted the new iconographic programme for the paintings in the hall, assisted by the Camaldolese monk Girolamo de' Bardi, who in 1587 published a description of it.

Sala del Maggior Consiglio, ceiling, Jacopo Palma Giovane, *Venice Crowned by Victory Welcomes the Subject Provinces*, 1582-1584

Sala del Maggior Consiglio, Domenico Tintoretto, *Portrait of Doge Andrea Dandolo and damnatio memoriae of Doge Marino Falier*, 1580-1590

The paintings set in the ceiling, however, were installed by 1584. These include chiaroscuri with historic events and trophies of war flanked by more complex works by famous artists. The grand, spectacular *Triumph of Venice* by Paolo Veronese is positioned above the tribunal, followed by *Doge Nicolò da Ponte, in the Presence of Venice, Receiving Tribute from the Ambassadors of the Subject Cities* in a central position, by Jacopo Tintoretto and assistants, and, further on, *Venice Crowned by Victory Welcomes the Subject Provinces* by Palma Giovane. The twelve compartments at the sides present scenes of wartime heroism, ferocious encounters won by *condottieri* and by militias in the service of the Serenissima: *The Taking of Izmir* (1471) and *The Defence of Scutari* (1474) by Veronese, *The Battle of Casalmaggiore* (1446) and *The Battle of Polesella* (1482-1484) by Francesco Bassano, *The Battle of Riva* (1440), *The Battle of Argenta* (1482), *The Defence of Brescia* (1438) and *The Battle of Gallipoli* (1494) by the workshop of Tintoretto (Antonio Aliense?), *The Battle of Maclodio* (1426) and *The Battle of Cadore* (1508) again by Bassano, *The Victory of Cremona* (1427) and *Andrea Gritti Wins Back Padua* (1510) by Palma Giovane.

The high fascia of the walls is surrounded on three sides by a frieze in which Domenico Tintoretto painted the portraits of the doges who ruled between 804 and 1556, from Oberlerio Antenoreo to Francesco Venier, making copies taken from real portraits or inventing those for the earlier figures. The only one missing is that of Marino Falier, the doge condemned to death in 1355 for conspiracy against the State, subject to *damnatio memoriae* as a permanent warning; the black drapery carries the words 'HIC EST LOCUS MARINI FALETRO DECAPITATI

Sala dello Scrutinio,

Sala dello Scrutinio,
Jacopo Palma
Giovane,
Last Judgement,
1594-1595

PRO CRIMINIBUS' (this is the place of Marino Falier, beheaded for the crimes he committed).

The narrative developed in the canvases along the sides of the hall is concentrated into two primary themes. This is a genuine compendium of late-sixteenth-century Venetian painting that includes works by Carlo and Gabriele Caliari, Domenico Tintoretto, Francesco and Leandro Bassano, Paolo Fiammingo, Andrea Vicentino, Palma Giovane, Federico Zuccari, Girolamo Gambarato, Giulio dal Moro, Jean Le Clerc, Antonio Aliense and Veronese. There are twelve episodes from the stories of Alessandro III and Frederick Barbarossa towards the courtyard, legitimising some attributes of ducal authority. This was a clever manipulation of historic reality for propaganda purposes, whose iconography is taken up from previous decorative cycles. The urban views of Venice are interesting, such as that of the Doge's Palace in the painting with *Pope Alexander III Consigning the Sword to Doge Sebastiano Ziani* by Francesco Bassano. The exploits of the fourth crusade (1202-1204) are lined up rather between the windows on the quay side, presenting solemn moments and excited scenes of assault, like *The Conquest of Zara* by Andrea Vicentino and *The Taking of Con-*

stantinople by Domenico Tintoretto. At the end, *The Victory over the Genoese at Chioggia* (1380) by Carlo and Gabriele Caliari is the only record of that fourteenth-century war.

The tribunal wall is entirely covered by the enormous painting of *Paradise*. A new work, though of the same subject, had been planned to replace the aging fresco by Guariento even before the fire. Only during the restoration works to the hall, however, was a kind of competition held to identify a painter for the work, resulting in Jacopo Tintoretto being nominated in 1588 (there are numerous sketches, also by the other participants, in various European and American museums). The elderly master conceived the composition and transferred the preparatory drawings to sections of canvas in the vast space of the Scuola Grande della Misericordia. These were subsequently reassembled and finished in the Maggior Consiglio, mainly by his son Domenico. The celestial circles contain a host of saints, blessed and angels, drawing towards the apex of the empyrean, where the divine light enfolds the Virgin and Christ: Venice – the allusion is obvious – is considered to be invested with a heavenly mission and, with the power of images, is presented as heaven on Earth.

Sala dello Scrutinio,
Andrea Vicentino,
Battle of Lepanto,
1595-1605

Sala dello Scrutinio

Access to the Sala dello Scrutinio (Voting Chamber), in the fifteenth-century section of the Doge's Palace, is by the connecting hallway or the nearby room where the Quarantia Civil Nuova met, decorated with seventeenth-century allegorical paintings by Antonio del Foler, Filippo Zaniberti and Giovanni Battista Lorenzetti.

Prior to being used only for voting procedures (1532), this hall held the precious codices that Francesco Petrarch and Cardinal Bessarion had donated to the Serenissima, subsequently moved to the Marciana Library on the other side of the Piazzetta. The fire of 1577 destroyed the works of art then in the hall, particularly the coffered ceiling designed by Sebastiano Serlio with compartments painted by Pordenone, and some canvases by Jacopo Tintoretto, including a recent portrayal of the Battle of Lepanto, which had taken place only six years before. The restorations, though quickly decided, continued until the end of the century.

The ceiling was designed by Cristoforo Sorte, already at work in the Senato and the Maggior Consiglio, and is little different from the previous models, showing the usual range of festoons, scrolls, herms and 'nudes' against a blue background covered with vegetal forms. The monk Girolamo de' Bardi was once again asked to provide the iconographic programme, also for the walls, but this was subject to alterations and changes over time with a great many later additions. The central canvases show some glorious exploits of early Venetians, among Virtues and allegorical figures, which, starting from the wall nearest the basilica, are *The Victory over the Pisans at Rhodes* (1098) by Andrea Vicentino, *The Conquest of Acre* (1256) by Francesco Monte-mezzano, *The Victory over the Genoese at Trapani* (1265) by Camillo Ballini, *The Conquest of Caffa* (1296) by Giulio dal Moro and *The De–*

Sala dello Scrutinio, Jacopo Tintoretto and assistants, *Battle of Zara*, 1584-1587

Sala dello Scrutinio, Jacopo Tintoretto and assistants, *Battle of Zara*, detail, 1584-1587

feat of Padua and Francesco da Carrara (1405), a notable nocturnal work by Francesco Bassano. The smaller ovals contain heroic episodes from the lives of four doges painted by Giulio dal Moro, Antonio Aliense and Nicolò Bambini.

Beneath the frieze with the ducal portraits, from Lorenzo Priuli (1556-1559) to Ludovico Manin (1789-1797) by Domenico Tintoretto and

Sala dello Scrutinio,
Pietro Liberi,
*The Victory over
the Turks at the
Dardanelles,*
1659-1664

Sala dello Scrutinio,
ceiling, Francesco
Bassano, *The
Defeat of Padua
and Francesco da
Carrara,* 1583-1584

contemporary artists of the doges, there are allegories and numerous paintings showing wartime events from between the tenth and seventeenth centuries, beginning with the clashes, shrouded in legend, with the French king Pippin the Short. Apart from the works by Aliense, Sante Peranda, Marco Vecellio and Pietro Bellotti, the three big paintings on the wall towards the courtyard deserve special mention: the lively *Battle of Zara* (1346) by Jacopo Tintoretto and assistants, the animated *Battle of Lepanto* (1571) by Andrea Vicentino, and *The Victory over the Turks at the Dardanelles* (1656) by Pietro Liberi, noteworthy for the enormous slave fighting in the foreground.

The *Last Judgement* by Palma Giovane (1594-1595) in the Sala dello Scrutinio corresponds to the *Paradise* in the Maggior Consiglio. Indeed, it may be counted among the best works by this artist in terms of its compositional orchestration and the power of the colours. The coat of arms of Doge Francesco Foscari (1423-1457) appears on the stone in the centre with Latin inscriptions. The doorway on the opposite side, which opens up onto the Scala Foscara and gives access to the loggias, was adapted by the architect Antonio Gaspari shortly after 1694 into a triumphal arch in classical Roman style in honour of Doge Francesco Morosini, who conquered the Peloponnese during a glorious military campaign to which the six paintings by Gregorio Lazzarini allude.

The visit to the palace may be continued in the direction of the prisons and the last institutional rooms by returning to the Sala del Maggior Consiglio.

Towards the Prisons

A narrow passage that opens up in the corner of the Maggior Consiglio overlooking the courtyard beside the *Paradise* gives access to a corridor that ends at the entrance to the doge's apartment. However, the route turns aside into some side rooms that lead to the Ponte dei Sospiri and the mighty prison building on the other side of the canal. There were several places of detention in the Doge's Palace over the centuries, mainly concentrated on the ground floor in appalling, restricted spaces that must have considerably aggravated the offender's punishment. Only two areas of detention remained after construction of the prisons, however: the *Pozzi* (Wells), near the canal, which were damp, unlit, unhealthy and with vaults so low that it was not possible to stand upright, and the *Piombi* (Leads) in the attic, named after the sheets of roofing metal. The temperature in these cells reserved for special prisoners reached extreme levels that made them intolerable both in summer and winter.

Sale della Quarantia Criminale e dei Cuoi

Older than the Quarantia Civile, the Quarantia Criminale had judicial power, deciding at appeal level on penal cases. It was directed by three officials who, along with the doge and his councillors, made up the Serenissima Signoria. All the furnishings and decorations apart from the seventeenth-century wooden stalls were removed after the fall of the Republic.

As the adjacent room acted as an archive, it is likely that the walls were covered with shelving and cabinets for papers, so the present furniture and the covering in *cuoridoro*, typically Venetian ornamental panels of gilt leather, do not belong to the room's original furnishings. There must have been a table or desk in the middle of the room, given that it was used by the magistracy of the three Presidenti sopra Uffici, elected from among the Quaranta al Criminal with responsibility for regulating the entire civil ministry of the Republic.

Sala del Magistrato alle Leggi, Quentin Metsys, *Christ Mocked*, early 16th century

Sala del Magistrato alle Leggi

Set up in 1553, the three registrars and executors of the laws and orders pertaining to the offices of San Marco and Rialto had to ensure that the laws governing the legal profession were respected, while also allowing jurisconsults and notaries to exercise their professions. They also had the faculty of deciding in cases between close relatives and acting as guarantors that the dictates of wills were observed. The Collegio dei Venti Savi (College of Twenty Ministers) selected from among the Quaranta also met in this room. Their responsibility in controversies regarding small sums of money made their role an essential one in a city founded on trade.

The fireplace between the windows bears the coat of arms of the Venier house, which produced two doges in the sixteenth century: Francesco (1554-1556) and Sebastiano (1577-1578). Significant works of Flemish art adorn the walls: the *Inferno* signed by the monogram painter JS, *Christ Mocked* by Quentin Metsys and two triptychs signed by Hieronymus Bosch, long held in the Sala dei Tre Capi of the Consilio dei Dieci. They were left to the Republic along with other treasures in 1523 by the distinguished collector Cardinal Domenico Grimani. The early *Triptych of Saint Julia* and the later *Triptych of Hermit Saints*, dating from the start of the sixteenth century, show the miniaturist skills and lively imagination of the originally Dutch painter, renowned for his scenes crowded with monsters; devilish,

Sala del Magistrato
alle Leggi,
Monogram painter
J.S., *Inferno*, first
half of 16th century

The Bridge of Sighs

frightening creatures that evoke the cruelty of the world, contrasted by the salvic power of faith in God.

The Ponte dei Sospiri

The narrow steps of a staircase from the nearby room lead to a confined passageway that crosses the famous Ponte dei Sospiri (Bridge of Sighs), a name already in use in the late eighteenth century. The enclosed bridge connecting the palace and the new prisons is distinguished by the highly expressive play of white facades in Istrian stone crowned by a mixtilinear pediment. The same material is used for the windows, through which many of the condemned gazed on the glimmering waters of the lagoon for the last time, breathing sighs of farewell. The joins between the ashlars of the arch are hidden by grotesque masks, while the geometries of the squares above highlight the bas-relief portraying *Justice* and the coat of arms of Doge Marino Grimani (1595-1605). The construction works ended around 1602 under the supervision of Manopola, who succeeded the *proti* Antonio da Ponte and Antonio Contin as building site director.

The double internal corridor of the Bridge of Sighs, seen from the Stanza di Sbocco in the New Prisons

The New Prisons

Construction work on the new building on the other side of the canal began in 1580, with the precise aim of creating a place devoted entirely to confinement so that most of the prisoners could be moved

A corridor in the New Prisons

out of the insanitary cells in the Doge's Palace. The new building was conceived to meet functional criteria, with a large number of openings and fairly spacious rooms in which the prisoners could better endure their detention. Rusticated blocks of Istrian stone make up the canal facade and other elevations, while the ashlared front facing the quay is marked by a portico with seven arches and, at the upper level, colossal windows and columns. The Collegio dei Signori di Notte al Criminal, consisting of six magistrates, the same number as there are *sestieri* (districts) in Venice, met in the room above the loggia. They kept a check on public order during the night and prosecuted crimes of theft, assault and homicide.

The new prisons, whose construction was partly financed by the issue of two public loans, were designed by the *proto* Antonio da Ponte, Zamaria de' Piombi and Zaccaria Briani, the server of a life sentence who received three years' remission in return for his contribution. But the works were not completed until the start of the seventeenth century, under the direction of Antonio Contin. The prison areas are arranged on three floors of simple design around a courtyard. A corridor leads from the Ponte dei Sospiri along the perimeter walls then crossing between two groups of cells. Many of the cells are still lined with thick planks of larch, crossed and nailed to the walls, floor and vault to offer protection against the damp. Several inscriptions scratched into the plaster of some rooms or traced with lamp-

New Prisons,
Cell interior

Sala dei Censori

black offer evidence of the many prisoners who were held here over the years.

On reaching the courtyard, the route passes through a door with the epigraph LE PREGION FORTE on the architrave, then goes up to a big room on the third floor where numerous archaeological finds are displayed. These were found during excavations in various parts of the city and lagoon: Malamocco, the State Archives at the Frari, the church of San Lorenzo in Castello, the New Prisons, the Doge's Palace and the bell tower of Saint Mark, which collapsed in 1902. The display cases contain fragments of Roman and high Medieval amphorae, the remains of a meal (animal bones, mollusc shells) and earthenware shards of bowls, plates and tankards dating from various periods, produced locally and in Byzantium, the Middle East and Moorish Spain. From here the tour returns to the rooms of some important magistracies on the loggia floor of the Doge's Palace.

Sala dei Censori

The passageway through the Ponte dei Sospiri in the opposite direction, on the side facing the basin, leads to the room where the censors met. This magistracy was set up in 1517 and consisted of two members nominated by the Maggior Consiglio. They kept a check on voting to prevent rigging, but also decided on questions relating to the pay of servants, to gambling, to crimes committed by gondoliers and, from the eighteenth century, also had jurisdiction over glassmaking. Their decisions were valid only if unanimous, for obvious numerical reasons. The coats of arms of the censors in office from the year of their constitution to 1632 are displayed along the wooden cornice that runs

Sala dell'Avogaria, Jacopo Tintoretto, *The Risen Christ with Avogadori Francesco Pisani, Michele Bon and Ottaviano Valier,* c. 1571

Sala dell'Avogaria, Leandro Bassano, *The Virgin and Child Worshipped by Three Avogadori,* 1604

above the panelling, while higher up there is a series of canvases with group portraits of members of the magistracy, most of which are by Domenico Tintoretto.

Sala degli Avogadori di Comun

The Avogaria (legal office) which may have already existed in the twelfth century, was primarily responsible for safeguarding the assets of the Comune and deciding in trials between the exchequer and the citizen; it later took on an important role in the State's complex political machine, acquiring the right to challenge decisions taken in the Maggior Consiglio, the Senato and the Consiglio dei Dieci, where at least one *avogadore* (lawyer) had to be present to ensure full respect for the law. Its responsibilities varied from auditing the finances of the offices of San Marco and Rialto to implementing confiscations decided by the Ten and replacing other magistracies in holiday periods. The three *avogadori* normally wore purple togas, but exchanged these for crimson ones on solemn occasions.

The current appearance of the room does not correspond to the original layout in the time of the Republic, having been subject to alterations and demolitions during works to the palace in the nineteenth century. The big painting in the centre of the wall towards the Sala dei Censori is by Jacopo Tintoretto and depicts *The Risen Christ with Avogadori Francesco Pisani, Michele Bon and Ottaviano Valier* (c. 1571). It is surrounded by other portraits, some of which include religious images dating from the start of the eighteenth century by painters who specialised in this genre: Domenico Tintoretto, Leandro Bassano, Tiberio Tinelli and Sebastiano Bombelli.

Sala dello Scrigno

The task of keeping a special register of all the families belonging to the Venetian nobility, the so-called Golden Book, was assigned to the *avogadori* in 1319. All marriages and births had to be inscribed in this so that the legitimacy of entry into the Maggior Consiglio by young nobles could be checked. There was a similar book, the Silver Book, for registering indigenous citizens, a social class that enjoyed certain privileges such as the opportunity of taking up important posts in the public administration and conducting foreign trade. The eighteenth-century cabinets with gilt decorations on a white ground in the hallway created beneath the Scala d'Oro held the precious volumes and all papers relating to the processes of recognising noble titles and citizenship.

There are numerous portraits in the room, including some notable paintings from the seventeenth and eighteenth centuries by Nicolas Régnier, Alessandro Longhi, Vincenzo Guarana and anonymous artists.

Sala dei Provveditori alla Milizia da Mar

The Magistratura dei Provveditori or Presidenti alla Milizia da Mar (Ship Chandlers) was set up in the mid-sixteenth century with a variable number of members, reduced to three in 1585. This office was responsible for fitting out the galleys in the Venetian fleet and enlisting seamen. The trade corporations of Venice and its subject cities were at first required to supply a certain number of men to crew the ships after payment of a *tansa* for this purpose.

The room still contains the original sixteenth-century wooden panelling, while the wrought iron wall lamps decorated with leaves and floral corollas are from the eighteenth century; the religious paintings by an anonymous painter of the Tiepolo school date from the same period.

Final section of the tour

The tour of the palace ends in the room currently used as a bookshop, which was once the chancellery where the college of notaries used to meet. The room next door known as the Sala della Bolla Ducale (Room of the Ducal Bull) was occupied by a magistrate, the *bollador*, who validated all papers by affixing an authorisation stamp. The doorway crowned by the coat of arms of Doge Leonardo Loredan (1501-1521) leads back to the loggia, where a stone recording the visit of Henry III to Venice can be seen set in a rich mannerist frame, a masterpiece by Alessandro Vittoria, behind the Giganti. The Scala dei Senatori then leads down to the courtyard of the same name, while the passage from the bookshop gives access to the cafe below in the rooms of the ancient kitchens. The Foscari arch and reception hall, the grandiose, solemn entrance to the Doge's Palace, leads to the Gothic Porta della Carta from where visitors can continue discovering the many extraordinary places that make Venice unique.

The Secret Itinerary

The Secret Itinerary, a separately booked, escorted tour, offers the chance to discover parts of the palace that are less official, but not without interest and intrigue: offices where the administrative life of the Republic was conducted, places used for detention or torture, rooms that housed extremely feared magistrates watching over State security. Each step leads into the historic past of the Serenissima, gradually revealing the mechanisms that regulated its complex bureaucratic system and exercise of judicial power.

After the doorway in the Atrio Quadrato facing the entrance to the institutional rooms, there is a narrow, hushed corridor with partitions consisting of simple tables or thin walls. On the right, tiny communicating offices are lit by the big Renaissance windows that look onto the courtyard, divided in half by the wooden floor. The *Notaio Ducale*, assistant to numerous magistrates as secretary, sat here with the *Deputato alla Secreta del Consiglio dei Dieci*, responsible for an archive of confidential deeds, along with papers relating to cases prepared by the Ten.

A staircase leads to the mezzanine and the room of the *Cancelliere Grande*, which is fairly modest considering the dignity of this official, called on to supervise the entire Venetian public administration. Appointed from the class of indigenous citizens, he was nominated for life by the Maggior Consiglio and enjoyed all the prerogatives of the patricians, though without any deliberative vote in the assemblies he attended. Solemn state rites that were otherwise reserved solely for the doge and the patriarch were performed on his death. The *Segretario alle Voci* occupied the adjoining room, responsible for custody of the registers of elections held in the Maggior Consiglio and Senato.

The continuation of the staircase leads to the large Sala della Cancelleria Superiore, corresponding to the Atrio Quadrato and the well of the Scala d'Oro. The walls are entirely covered by wooden cabinets dating from the eighteenth century, whose panels are painted with

A dormer window
in the attic

the coats of arms and names of the chancellors (the first to be recorded is Corrado de' Ducati, in office in 1268); the archives of the Signoria and the Collegio were kept here, as were registers of the laws enacted by the Maggior Consiglio and the deliberations of the Senato, and the papers necessary for carrying out everyday procedures. The secretary clerks worked at long tables that once stood beneath the wooden baluster.

The disturbing Sala della Tortura (Torture Room, or room of torment) is reached from the nearby offices of the *Reggente* and the *Vicereggente*, where confessions were wrung from the accused mainly by use of the rope method, which entailed tying the arms behind the back then raising them with a cord. Torture in Venice was always of a mild form, though, and was in any case abandoned from the seventeenth century. A series of narrow corridors connects the room, which is surrounded by big spaces on the gallery floor, too, to the area of the Piombi (Leads), a name deriving from the lead roofing plates. These six or seven cells in the attic were used for those awaiting sentence from the Consiglio dei Dieci or the Inquisitori di Stato. Several layers of nailed larch planks strengthened with sheets of iron did not, however, prevent the audacious escape in 1756 of Giacomo Casanova, who had been imprisoned for suspected espionage and cheating some nobles. After a failed first attempt, Casanova made a hole in the ceiling with the help of an accomplice and reached the roof. He then re-entered

Sala della Cancelleria Superiore

The torture room

the palace through a dormer window, arriving in the Atrio Quadrato at dawn after various mishaps. A guard then mistook him for a visitor who had been inadvertently locked in on the second floor the night before and opened the doors, allowing him to get out and win his freedom. In the Austrian Lombardy-Veneto period these areas continued to be used as a prison; Silvio Pellico was held here in 1821. The rooms above those of the Armeria, in the corner between the canal and the quay, have some display cases with swords, halberds, cuirasses, crossbows, pistols and other arms. They are next to the attic of the Maggior Consiglio where it is possible to admire the stout, sixteenth-century beams put up by the expert craftsmen of the Arsenale to support the ceiling and the canvases set into it.

A double flight goes down to the second floor from the Piombi, letting into the Sala degli Inquisitori di Stato (State Inquisitors Room), an office set up in 1539 under the name of 'inquisitors against informers'. The magistrates (a ducal councillor and two members chosen from the Ten) pronounced summary sentences that were immediately effective, punishing crimes that endangered State security, political coups, slandering of the government and illegal relations with foreign emissaries. The ceiling compartments were painted by Jacopo Tintoretto in 1566-1567: the criteria and principles that the judges had to respect in formulating their verdicts are suggested in the lateral paintings with *Faith, Law, Justice* and *Concord*, while *The Return of the Prodigal Son* in the central octagon eloquently shows the aims of the inquisitors' deliberations.

The governing board of the Consiglio dei Dieci sat in the adjacent Sala di Tre Capi; these three nobles, who remained in office for one month, heard the accused, examined the truthfulness of the facts, presented cases to the assembly and informed the Signoria and the decemvirs of the most urgent provisions to be taken. The decoration of the room includes a big fireplace designed by Jacopo Sansovino with the coat of arms of Doge Marcantonio Trevisan (1553-1554), with two caryatids sculpted by Pietro da Salò and Danese Cattaneo and, on the chimney breast, a seventeenth-century wooden bas-relief portraying *Venice in the Form of Justice*, with scales and sceptre. Commemorative aims are concealed in the ceiling canvases, painted by the same artists who worked in the room of the Consiglio dei Dieci: the middle insert with *Virtue Frees Time, Truth and Innocence from Evil and Envy* is by Giambattista Zelotti, and the monochromes around it by Giambattista Ponchino – *Justice Conquers Rebellion* and *Faith Prevails over Heresy* – and Paolo Veronese – *Virtue Conquers Evil* and *Nemesis Triumphs over Sin*.

To the right of the corridor where the tour began is the passage leading to the Sala della Bussola and staircase that gives access to the other floors of the palace; further on there is a secret passage that opens directly into the semi-circular tribune of the Consiglio dei Dieci.

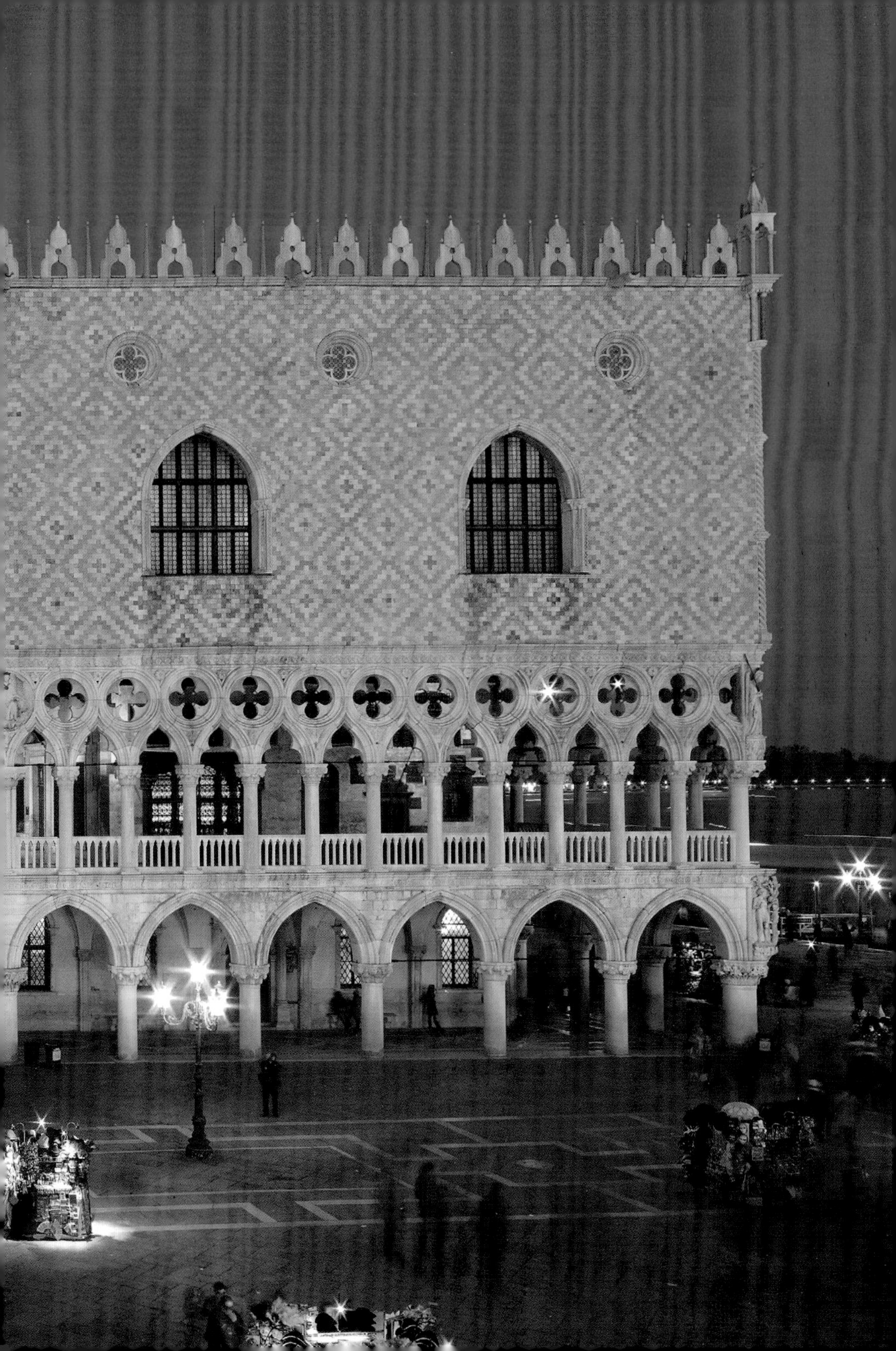

The Doges

697-717	Paolo Lucio Anafesto
717-726	Marcello Tegalliano
726-737	Orso Ipato
737-742	Periodo dei *Magistri militum* annuali
742-755	Teodato Ipato
755-756	Galla Lupanio
756-764	Domenico Monegario
764-787	Maurizio Galbaio
787-804	Giovanni Galbaio
804-810	Obelerio Antenoreo
810-827	Agnello Partecipazio
827-829	Giustiniano Partecipazio
829-836	Giovanni I Partecipazio
836-864	Pietro Tradonico
864-881	Orso I Partecipazio
881-887	Giovanni II Partecipazio
887	Pietro I Candiano
888-912	Pietro Tribuno
912-932	Orso II Partecipazio
932-939	Pietro II Candiano
939-942	Pietro Partecipazio
942-959	Pietro III Candiano
959-976	Pietro IV Candiano
976-978	Pietro I Orseolo
978-979	Vitale Candiano
979-991	Tribuno Memmo
991-1008	Pietro II Orseolo
1008-1026	Ottone Orseolo
1026-1032	Pietro Centranico
1032-1042	Domenico Flabanico
1043-1070	Domenico Contarini
1071-1084	Domenico Selvo
1084-1096	Vitale Falier
1096-1102	Vitale I Michiel
1102-1118	Ordelaffo Falier
1118-1130	Domenico Michiel
1130-1148	Pietro Polani
1148-1156	Domenico Morosini
1156-1172	Vitale II Michiel
1172-1178	Sebastiano Ziani
1178-1192	Orio Malipiero
1192-1205	Enrico Dandolo
1205-1229	Pietro Ziani
1229-1249	Jacopo Tiepolo
1249-1253	Marino Morosini
1253-1268	Ranieri Zen
1268-1275	Lorenzo Tiepolo
1275-1280	Jacopo Contarini
1280-1289	Giovanni Dandolo
1289-1311	Pietro Gradenigo
1311-1312	Marino Zorzi
1312-1328	Giovanni Soranzo
1329-1339	Francesco Dandolo
1339-1342	Bartolomeo Gradenigo
1343-1354	Andrea Dandolo
1354-1355	Marino Falier
1355-1356	Giovanni Gradenigo
1356-1361	Giovanni Dolfin
1361-1365	Lorenzo Celsi
1365-1368	Marco Corner
1368-1382	Andrea Contarini
1382	Michele Morosini
1382-1400	Antonio Venier
1400-1413	Michele Steno
1414-1423	Tommaso Mocenigo
1423-1457	Francesco Foscari
1457-1462	Pasquale Malipiero
1462-1471	Cristoforo Moro
1471-1473	Nicolò Tron
1473-1474	Nicolò Marcello
1474-1476	Pietro Mocenigo
1476-1478	Andrea Vendramin
1478-1485	Giovanni Mocenigo
1485-1486	Marco Barbarigo
1486-1501	Agostino Barbarigo
1501-1521	Leonardo Loredan
1521-1523	Antonio Grimani
1523-1538	Andrea Gritti
1539-1545	Pietro Lando
1545-1553	Francesco Donà
1553-1554	Marcantonio Trevisan
1554-1556	Francesco Venier
1556-1559	Lorenzo Priuli
1559-1567	Girolamo Priuli
1567-1570	Pietro Loredan
1570-1577	Alvise I Mocenigo
1577-1578	Sebastiano Venier
1578-1585	Nicolò da Ponte
1585-1595	Pasquale Cicogna
1595-1605	Marino Grimani
1606-1612	Leonardo Donà
1612-1615	Marcantonio Memmo
1615-1618	Giovanni Bembo
1618	Nicolò Donà
1618-1623	Antonio Priuli
1623-1624	Francesco Contarini
1625-1629	Giovanni I Corner
1630-1631	Nicolò Contarini
1631-1646	Francesco Erizzo
1646-1655	Francesco Molin
1655-1656	Carlo Contarini
1656	Francesco Corner
1656-1658	Bertucci Valier
1658-1659	Giovanni Pesaro
1659-1675	Domenico Contarini
1675-1676	Nicolò Sagredo
1676-1684	Alvise Contarini
1684-1688	Marcantonio Giustinian
1688-1694	Francesco Morosini
1694-1700	Silvestro Valier
1700-1709	Alvise II Mocenigo
1709-1722	Giovanni II Corner
1722-1732	Alvise III Mocenigo
1732-1735	Carlo Ruzini
1735-1741	Alvise Pisani
1741-1752	Pietro Grimani
1752-1762	Francesco Loredan
1762-1763	Marco Foscarini
1763-1778	Alvise IV Mocenigo
1779-1789	Paolo Renier
1789-1797	Ludovico Manin

Lazzaro Bastiani,
Doge Francesco Foscari, Venice,
Museo Correr

137

Chronology

421
According to legend, Venice is founded on Annunciation Day (25 March).

567
The Exarchate of Italy is established, based in Ravenna, and a tribune appointed to rule over maritime Venice.

568-569
Alboin leads the Langobard invasion of Italy.

589
A massive flood changes the geography of the lagoon.

697
Tradition identifies the first *dux* as Paoluccio Anafesto da Eraclea.

737-741
After the assassination of Doge Orso Ipato, rule passes to the annually nominated *magistri militum*.

742
Teodato Ipato is proclaimed doge and moves to Malamocco.

810
The French army of Pepin, son of Charlemagne, is defeated by Agnello Partecipazio, who moves the ducal residence to Rivoalto.

828
The relics of Saint Mark arrive in Venice, having been stolen from Alexandria, Egypt, by the merchants Bono da Malamocco and Rustico da Torcello.

976
Doge Pietro IV Candiano and his son die during an uprising in which the palace is burned.

1000
The Venetian fleet commanded by Doge Pietro Orseolo, flying the flag of Saint Mark for the first time, defeats the Slav pirates threatening the coasts of Istria and Dalmatia (which gave rise to the *Festa della Sensa*).

1082
Having been assisted by Venice in the fight against the Normans, the Byzantine emperor grants the city generous trading privileges.

1094
St Mark's Basilica is consecrated in the presence of the Holy Roman Emperor Henry IV.

1096-1099
The first crusade takes place to return the Holy Land to Christianity. Despite its late participation, the Venetians ensure themselves the best trading markets in the new states of the Near East.

1143
The *Comune Veneciarum* is founded.

1172
The Maggior Consiglio is founded.

1172-1178
Doge Sebastiano Ziani promotes numerous works in the piazza, which is enlarged and surrounded by new buildings; the walls around the Doge's Palace are replaced with edifices in Byzantine style with porticoes and loggias.

1177
Pope Alexander III is reconciled with Emperor Frederick Barbarossa under the gilt domes of the basilica, thanks to the intercession of Doge Ziani.

1192
Enrico Dandolo is the first doge to swear observance of the *promissione ducale*.

1202-1204
The Venetians divert the fourth crusade from the conquest of Jerusalem to subdue the rebel city of Zara and attack Constantinople, which is sacked (the bronze horses of Saint Mark were part of the booty). Doge Dandolo obtains the title of 'Lord of a Quarter and Half a Quarter of the Roman Empire'.

1211
The island of Candia (Crete) is annexed to Venetian control.

1229
The founding of the Consiglio dei Pregadi (or Senate) is generally dated to this year.

1255-1270
The Venetians and Genoese fight in the war of San Saba for control of eastern trade.

1271
Marco Polo leaves for Cathay; he was to return to Venice in 1295.

1284
The first gold ducat is minted, which was to be known as the zecchino (sequin) from 1554.

1293-1299
The republics of Venice and Genoa engage in a new armed conflict. Marco Polo is taken prisoner during the battle of Curzola (1298).

1297
Admission to the Maggior Consiglio is restricted by the so-called *serrata* (28 February).

1310
The plot hatched by Baiamonte Tiepolo and Marco Querini is quelled (14 June). The Consiglio dei Dieci is set up to try the culprits.

1339
Treviso is taken from the Scaligeri; it was to pass into permanent Venetian control in 1388.

1340
Construction begins on the wing of the Doge's Palace housing the Great Council Chamber.

1348
The black plague begins to spread in Venice in March, killing half the population.

1355
Doge Marino Falier is beheaded for conspiracy and attempted overthrow of republican rule (17 April). His portrait in the Great Council Chamber was erased and replaced by a black drape in 1366 by decree of the Consiglio dei Dieci.

1368-1370
The Venetians wage the war of Trieste to ensure the security of the Adriatic trade routes.

1378-1381
The war of Chioggia, which ends with the peace of Turin (8 August 1381), marks the decline of the Republic of Genoa, which was never again to pose a threat to the Serenissima.

1392
Restrictions are imposed on the use of horses in Venice.

1404-1405
The Serenissima extends its rule to Vicenza, Verona and Padua.

1420
The patriarch of Aquileia is forced to give up his role of *potestà* over Istria and Friuli.

1426-1433
Hostilities with Milan win Venice the Lombard cities of Brescia and Bergamo.

1449
The flag of St Mark flies over Crema, too.

1454
The peace of Lodi confirms Venetian rule through to Adda.

1457
Doge Francesco Foscari is forced to abdicate.

1469
Negroponte falls into Turkish hands.

1482-1484
The war of Ferrara, or the Salt war, ends with the permanent occupation of Rovigo and declaration of the Republic's southern border along the line of the Po.

1483
On 14 September a fire destroys the east wing of the Doge's Palace, which is rebuilt in Renaissance style.

1489
Caterina Corner, widow of the last king, James of Lusignan, cedes the island of Cyprus to the Republic.

1492
Christopher Columbus discovers America, launching a series of explorations that were to open up new routes and thus weaken trade in the Mediterranean.

1499-1503
In the course of the conflict with the Ottoman Empire, Venice loses numerous possessions in Greece and the Aegean.

1509
The Venetian army is defeated at Agnadello by the united powers of the League of Cambrai (the Empire, Spain, France, the Papacy and other Italian lordships), and the enemy troops advance as far as Mestre. In subsequent years, marked by a constant change of alliances, the Republic gradually recovered its rule over the mainland cities.

1515
Venice forms an alliance with France and defeats the imperial and Swiss soldiers on the battlefield of Marignano.

1537-1540
The Turks continue encroaching on Venetian possessions in Greece.

1559
Spanish and Austrian rule in Italy is definitively sanctioned by the peace of Cateau-Cambrésis.

1570-1571
Cyprus is taken by the Ottomans, who massacre the defenders of Famagosta, the last Venetian bulwark.

1571
On 7 October, Saint Justine's Day, the fleet of the Holy League, uniting Venice, the Papacy and Spain, annihilates the Ottoman navy in the waters of Lepanto.

1573
Despite the victory of Lepanto, Venice is forced to give up Cyprus.

1574
Fire seriously damages some rooms in the Doge's Palace, including those of the Collegio and the Senato (11 May).

1577
The chambers of the Scrutinio and the Maggior Consiglio are destroyed by a terrible fire (20 December).

1588
The first stone of the Rialto Bridge is laid on 9 June.

1606-1607
Paul v imposes an interdict regarding questions of jurisdiction against Venice, which takes advice from Fra Paolo Sarpi.

1609
Galileo Galilei presents the telescope to the seigniory in the bell-tower of Saint Mark.

1615-1617
The Republic wages the war of Gradisca against Uskok pirates, armed by the Habsburgs of Austria.

1630
Plague breaks out in June and kills almost a third of the population.

1645-1669
The Turks invade Crete and besiege the capital, Candia, which surrenders after 22 years.

1683
The Ottoman army reaches the walls of Vienna.

1684-1689
Francesco Morosini leads the fight against the Turks and conquers the Morea, earning him the nickname 'Peloponnesiaco'.

1699
The peace of Carlowitz definitively assigns the Peloponnese to Venice.

1714-1718
Venice loses the Morea in a new conflict with the Ottomans, obtaining modest territorial concessions in Dalmatia and Albania with the peace of Passarowitz. Corfu is saved, defended in 1716 by Marshal Johann Matthias von der Schulenburg.

1723
The existing paving in St Mark's Square is laid to a design by Andrea Tirali.

1744
Work begins at the Lido on construction of the *murazzi* breakwater to protect the lagoon from sea storms.

1782
Pius VI comes to Venice, as do the heir princes of Russia under the name of the Counts of the North, and are celebrated with great shows.

1785-1786
Angelo Emo leads an expedition to northern Africa against the Barbary pirates.

1789
Ludovico Manin is elected, the 120th and last doge of the Republic of Venice. The French Revolution takes place in the same year.

1796
Napoleon embarks on the 'Italian campaign'.

1797
The Maggior Consiglio sits for the last time on 12 May, transferring power to a provisional municipality of Jacobin inspiration. Napoleon cedes the city to Austria with the treaty of Campoformido (17 October).

1799-1800
The conclave for the election of the new pope takes place at the island convent of San Giorgio Maggiore due to the French occupation of Rome; Pope Pius VII is elected.

1805
The empire cedes Venice to Napoleon after the defeat at Austerlitz.

1814
The Veneto goes back under Austrian rule.

1846
The lagoon railway bridge is completed and the first train leaves Venice in January.

1848-1849
The Austrians are driven out of Venice and the Republic of St Mark is set up under Daniele Manin.

1866
The Veneto is annexed to Italy.

Essential Bibliography

AA.VV., *Piazza San Marco, l'architettura, la storia, le funzioni*, Padova 1970

AA.VV., *Il Palazzo Ducale di Venezia*, Torino 1971

AA.VV., *Architettura e utopia nella Venezia del Cinquecento*, catalogo della mostra a Palazzo Ducale, Milano 1980

AA.VV., *Da Tiziano a El Greco. Per la storia del manierismo a Venezia*, catalogo della mostra a Palazzo Ducale, Milano 1981

AA.VV., *Venezia e la difesa del Levante. Da Lepanto a Candia 1570-1670*, catalogo della mostra a Palazzo Ducale, Venezia 1986

AA.VV., *Tiziano*, catalogo della mostra a Palazzo Ducale, Venezia 1990

AA.VV., *Storia di Venezia, dalle origini alla caduta della Serenissima*, 8 voll., Roma 1992-1998

AA.VV., *L'architettura gotica veneziana*, Venezia 2000

AA.VV., *Il Paradiso di Tintoretto. Un concorso per Palazzo Ducale*, catalogo della mostra a Palazzo Ducale, Milano 2006

M. Agazzi, *Platea Sancti Marci. I luoghi marciani dall'XI al XIII secolo e la formazione della piazza*, Venezia 1991

G. Bardi, *Dichiaratione di tutte le historie che si contengono ne i quadri posti nuovamente nelle Sale dello Scrutinio e del Gran Consiglio del Palagio Ducale della Serenissima Repubblica di Vinegia*, Venetia 1587

E. Bassi, *Palazzi di Venezia. Admiranda Urbis Venetae*, Venezia 1976

E. Bassi - E.R. Trincanato, *Il Palazzo Ducale nella storia e nell'arte di Venezia*, Milano 1965

G. Benzoni (a cura di), *I Dogi*, Milano 1982

P. Bettio (a cura di), *Lettera intorno al Palazzo Ducale e descrizione dei quadri nella sala del Gran Consiglio esistenti prima dell'incendio del 1577, pubblicate da Francesco Sansovino e riprodotte con illustrazioni*, Venezia 1829

G. Cozzi, *Repubblica di Venezia e Stati italiani*, Torino 1982

G. Cozzi (a cura di), *Stato, società e giustizia nella Repubblica Veneta (sec. XV-XVIII)*, Roma 1980

A. Da Mosto, *I Dogi di Venezia nella vita pubblica e privata*, Milano 1960²

W. Dorigo, *Venezia romanica*, Venezia 2003

U. Franzoi, *Storia e leggenda del Palazzo Ducale di Venezia*, Venezia 1982

U. Franzoi, *Itinerari segreti nel Palazzo Ducale di Venezia*, Treviso 1983

U. Franzoi, *L'Armeria del Palazzo Ducale a Venezia*, Treviso 1990

U. Franzoi, *Le prigioni di Palazzo Ducale a Venezia*, Milano 1997

U. Franzoi - T. Pignatti - W. Wolters, *Il Palazzo Ducale di Venezia*, Treviso 1990

U. Franzoi (a cura di), *Il serenissimo Doge*, Treviso 1986

D. Howard, *Jacopo Sansovino. Architecture and Patronage in Renaissance Venice*, New Haven 1987²

N.M. Knapton - G. Scarabello, *La Repubblica di Venezia nell'età moderna*, Torino 1992

F.C. Lane, *Storia di Venezia*, Torino 1978 (ed. originale *Venice. A Maritime Republic*, London 1973)

G. Lorenzetti, *Venezia e il suo estuario*, Trieste 2002 (I ed. Venezia 1926)

G. Lorenzi, *Monumenti per servire alla storia del Palazzo Ducale di Venezia*, Venezia 1868

A. Manno, *Il Poema del Tempo. I capitelli del Palazzo Ducale di Venezia. Storia e iconografia*, Venezia 1999

S. Mason Rinaldi, *Palma il Giovane. L'opera completa*, Milano 1984

R. Pallucchini - P. Rossi, *Tintoretto. Le opere sacre e profane*, Milano 1984

F. Pedrocco, *Tiziano*, Milano 2000

F. Pedrocco - T. Pignatti, *Veronese. Catalogo completo dei dipinti*, Firenze 1991

R. Polacco (a cura di), *Storia dell'arte marciana: l'architettura*, atti del Convegno Internazionale di Studi, Venezia 1997

L. Puppi, *Andrea Palladio*, Milano 1973

C. Rendina, *I Dogi. Storia e Segreti*, Roma 1981

G. Romanelli (a cura di), *Palazzo Ducale. Storia e restauri*, Verona 2004

J. Ruskin, *The Stones of Venice*, London 1851-1853

M. Sanudo, *De origine, situ et magistratibus urbis Venetae ovvero La città di Venetia (1493-1530)*, a cura di A. Caracciolo Aricò, Milano 1980

G. Scarabello, *Guida alla civiltà di Venezia*, Milano 1987

M. Tafuri, *Venezia e il Rinascimento. Religione, scienza, architettura*, Roma 1985

M. Tafuri (a cura di), *Renovatio Urbis. Venezia nell'età di Andrea Gritti*, Roma 1984

W. Wolters, *La scultura veneziana gotica (1300-1460)*, Venezia 1976

W. Wolters, *Storia e politica nei dipinti di Palazzo Ducale*, Venezia 1987 (ed. originale *Der Bilderschmuck des Dogenpalastes*, Stuttgart 1983)

F. Zanotto, *Il Palazzo Ducale di Venezia*, 4 voll., Venezia 1853-1861

Colour separation
Fotolito Veneta, San Martino Buonalbergo (Verona)

Printed by
Grafiche SIZ s.p.a., Campagnola (Verona)
for Marsilio Editori® s.p.a., Venezia

EDIZIONE   ANNO

10 9 8 7 6 5 4 3 2 1   2010 2011 2012 2013 2014